3/00

DATE DUE

11/19			
Nov 27, 2004			

Demco, Inc. 38-293

EXTRAORDINARY Women

Women EXTRAORDINARY

Women
Who
Changed
History

Edited by Catherine M. Edmonson

Adams Media Corporation
Holbrook, Massachusetts

Published by Adams Media Corporation
260 Center Street, Holbrook, MA 02343

ISBN: 1-58062-118-X

Printed in the United States of America.

J I H G F E D C B A

Library of Congress Cataloging-in-Publication Data
Extraordinary women / edited by Catherine M. Edmonson.
        p.   cm.
        ISBN 1-58062-118-X
1. Women—Biography. I. Edmonson, Catherine M.,
        CT3202.E98   1999
        920.72—dc21   98-51479
                             CIP

This publication is designed to provide accurate and authoritative information with regard
to the subject matter covered. It is sold with the understanding that the publisher is not
engaged in rendering legal, accounting, or other professional advice. If legal advice or
other expert assistance is required, the services of a competent professional person should
be sought.
    — From a *Declaration of Principles* jointly adopted by a Committee of the American Bar
                Association and a Committee of Publishers and Associations

Cover illustration ©Sandra Dionisi/SIS.

This book is available at quantity discounts for bulk purchases.
For information, call 1-800-872-5627 (in Massachusetts, 617-767-8100).

Visit our home page at http://www.adamsmedia.com

For Kate "My name's on it!" Kloosterman,
Wendy Breyer,
and
Emma Robertson

CONTENTS

x

Acknowledgments

Many thanks to the following people for their
assistance in completing this book:

Elise Bauman, Rick Dey,
Laura Morin, and Anne Weaver

INTRODUCTION

While many of the women in this book are famous for their accomplishments—for example, Eleanor Roosevelt, Margaret Sanger, Sojourner Truth, and Harriet Tubman—many more were chosen for the fact that they are *not* well known. Their contributions, great and small, were made in diverse fields ranging from health care to astronomy, from social work to art, from mathematics to prizewinning writing. Take Hessie Donahue, a vaudeville performer who inadvertently became the (unofficial) heavyweight boxing champion of the world when she knocked out prizefighter John Sullivan. Or Nellie Bly, a nineteenth-century writer who pretended to be insane in order to report on the inhumane conditions inside the notorious Blackwell's Island women's asylum. Famous, infamous, or merely overlooked, these women have all left their mark, and these inspirational true stories of their courage, ingenuity, and achievement are compelling evidence for their vital role in creating today's world.

GRACE ABBOTT, 1878–1939
AMERICAN SOCIAL ACTIVIST

Nebraska-born Grace Abbott was a public
administrator, educator, and reformer who fought
for immigrants' and children's rights. Having spent years
working with immigrants in Chicago's slums, she wrote *The
Immigrant and the Community* (1917), which helped raise
public awareness about the problems facing European
immigrants. Abbott was also a key figure in the field of
child labor legislation, and in 1921 she was appointed
director of the United States Children's Bureau in
Washington D.C., where she served for thirteen years. She
spent the final chapter of her life teaching social work at
the University of Chicago.

BELLA ABZUG, 1920–1998
AMERICAN POLITICIAN

Best known for her liberal activism, Abzug got her start in politics as a lawyer. Active in women's and civil rights, Abzug also established herself as one of the most antiwar members of Congress during the years she served there (1971–1976). She is credited with an impressive series of "first" accomplishments: she was the first to call on Richard Nixon to resign from the presidency; she cast one of the initial votes for the Equal Rights Amendment; she coauthored the Freedom of Information and Privacy Acts; and she cochaired the Women's Environmental Development Organization. Undaunted by her failure to be re-elected to Congress and the Senate, Abzug returned to her legal and activist career until her death.

ABIGAIL ADAMS, 1744–1818
AMERICAN FIRST LADY

Although best known as the wife of President John Adams, Abigail Adams's capacities went far beyond those of first lady. As her published letters show, she was a broad-minded feminist and abolitionist who was years ahead of her time. When she was not accompanying her husband abroad, she was advising him by letter, revealing her sharp political mind and sense for strategy as she managed family and business affairs at home. Well known for her staunch patriotism, Adams did step on a few toes while hosting political gatherings. She worked beyond her husband's terms as vice president and president to forge a better nation for all Americans.

Jane Addams, 1860–1935
American social reformer

In 1889, Addams cofounded Hull House, the first American settlement house, in a poor Chicago neighborhood. Hull House served as a model for other settlement houses, providing social services previously unavailable to the poor, including education, work for the unemployed, and child care. Addams was also a strong voice for women's rights, becoming president of the Women's International League for Peace and Freedom in 1919. Due in part to Addams's persistence, Illinois improved its welfare and child-labor laws, and established a juvenile court, mandatory school attendance, and workers' compensation. In 1931, she became the first American woman to receive the Nobel Peace Prize.

AGNODICE, FOURTH CENTURY B.C.
GREEK PHYSICIAN

Agnodice posed as a man in order to attend the lectures of the Greek physician Herophilus and to practice her specialty: gynecology. She achieved a good deal of fame for her competence in the new field while earning the enmity of other doctors. A trumped-up charge of corrupting the morals of women was brought against her, and in order to save her own life she revealed her true gender in court. She was then charged with practicing a profession limited by law to men—and was acquitted.

LOUISA MAY ALCOTT, 1832–1888
AMERICAN WRITER

Best known for her classic *Little Women*, Louisa May Alcott was also a strong supporter of the antislavery movement. Alcott grew up impoverished, largely because of her father's failed idealistic projects; her experiences are reflected in the stories of the March sisters in the largely autobiographical *Little Women*. Life began to look up for her, however, when her family moved to Concord, Massachusetts, where her neighbors included Ralph Waldo Emerson, Nathaniel Hawthorne, and Henry David Thoreau. As Alcott's name and work became better known, she also lent her support to the women's suffrage and temperance movements. She continued to write until her death in 1888.

HATTIE ELIZABETH ALEXANDER, 1901–1968

AMERICAN PHYSICIAN

Born in Baltimore, Alexander attended Johns Hopkins Medical School. During her internship at Columbia–Presbyterian Medical Center Babies' Hospital, meningococcal disease was so common that she came into daily contact with children dying of the infection. Using her background in bacteriology, she isolated the meningococcus antibody and formulated an antiserum. Before she made her contributions, the disease was always fatal in infants and untreatable in adults. She went on to head the Columbia–Presbyterian Medical Center's microbiological laboratory and the American Pediatrics Society. She conducted research in bacterial genetics, becoming one of the earliest to link DNA with genetic characteristics.

BLANCHE AMES, 1878–1969
AMERICAN ARTIST

A Smith College graduate, Ames married a botany instructor and applied her talent to her husband's work. Over seventeen years they published a series on orchids. Ames also cofounded the Birth Control League of Massachusetts, and she danced around the library table when an antisuffrage senator was defeated in a 1918 election. She invented several devices, including snares for catching low-flying enemy planes during World War II. In a letter to Blanche before their marriage, Oakes Ames wrote, "You and I are forming a contract . . . we have an equal voice." They managed not only to pursue their own very different careers, but also to enrich each other's work by their collaboration.

MARIAN ANDERSON, 1902–1993
AMERICAN SINGER

Anderson was the first African-American singer to break the color barrier at the Metropolitan Opera when she made her debut there in 1955. She attracted critical notice early in her career. Despite being acclaimed in her own country, she was able to obtain major engagements only in Europe, where she became a star. In the United States in 1939, the Daughters of the American Revolution canceled her contract to sing at Constitution Hall in Washington, D.C., when they found out that she was black. There was an outcry from public figures like Eleanor Roosevelt, who resigned from the DAR in protest. Following the controversy, Anderson was catapulted to the top of her profession, where she stayed until her retirement.

MAYA ANGELOU, 1928–
AMERICAN WRITER AND ACTRESS

Angelou is best known for her writing, from her autobiographical *I Know Why the Caged Bird Sings* (1970) through *Wouldn't Take Nothing for My Journey Now* (1993). Her enormously successful career has had some interesting twists along the way. She was San Francisco's first female, and first black, streetcar conductor in 1944, and had a (brief) stint as a madam in San Diego soon thereafter. In addition to her varied career as a singer, dancer, actress, director, and professor, Angelou gained more international attention when she read aloud the inaugural poem, "On the Pulse of Morning," she had written for President Clinton in 1993. She won the 1994 Grammy Award for Best Spoken Word.

Susan B. Anthony, 1820–1906

American suffragist

Though her achievements were finally honored in 1979, when she became the first woman to have her image on a U.S. government-issued coin, Susan B. Anthony's contributions to women's rights came a century earlier. In 1866, she cofounded the National Women's Suffrage Association. The daughter of a Quaker abolitionist, she devoted her life to the suffrage cause and became its recognized leader, even being arrested in 1872 for attempting to vote. She helped compile and edit the first four volumes of *The History of Woman Suffrage* (1881–1902).

MARIE ANTOINETTE, 1755–1793
QUEEN OF FRANCE

Austrian princess Marie Antoinette married Louis XVI of France in 1770. The marriage was unhappy, and by the time the pair ascended to the throne in 1774, Marie had little to do with her husband. At Versailles, a royal residence near Paris, her amusements included dressing up as a shepherdess and herding the royal sheep. Her spendthrift ways and foreign ancestry made her extremely unpopular with the public. In the early years of the French Revolution, Marie, Louis, and their children attempted to flee the country but were caught at Varennes. After conspiring to help Austria invade France to stop the revolution, Marie Antoinette was executed by guillotine for treason.

VIRGINIA APGAR, 1909–1974

AMERICAN SURGEON

Apgar is best known for devising the Newborn Scoring System, which evaluates general health in a newborn within one minute of birth. She was one of the first women to graduate from Columbia University's medical school. As director of anesthesiology at Columbia–Presbyterian, she was able to establish this specialty as a new academic department. After Apgar headed the department for eleven years, Columbia made her the first full professor of anesthesiology. Having attended more than 17,000 births, Apgar introduced her test in 1952. Measuring pulse, respiration, muscle tone, color, and reflexes, the system ensures that correctable problems do not go unnoticed. The "Apgar score" is now in use all over the world.

CORAZON AQUINO, 1933–

FORMER PRESIDENT OF THE PHILIPPINES

Aquino was president of the Philippines from 1986 to 1992. Her husband, Benigno S. Aquino, Jr., had been leader of the opposition until his assassination in 1983. She was educated in the United States and in addition to being a homemaker and mother, had served as her husband's liaison with the outside world during his imprisonment (1972–1980) for his opposition to President Ferdinand Marcos. Assuming leadership of the opposition, she ran against Marcos in 1985 and, after much nonviolent maneuvering and contesting of ballot results, won and forced him from office.

DIANE NEMEROV ARBUS, 1923–1971

AMERICAN PHOTOGRAPHER

Diane Nemerov Arbus's signature stark photographs depict physical "freaks," misfits, transvestites, and addicts. Though her images may seem grotesque to the casual observer, the New York native found in her subjects a particular dignity, which she sought to capture with a minimum of technique. Arbus won the prestigious Guggenheim Fellowship at forty, but her work was still not widely known when, at age forty-eight, she committed suicide. In 1972, when the Museum of Modern Art staged a major retrospective of her work, she became the object of a cult. Today Arbus is considered a major influence on modern photography.

ANNE ARMSTRONG, 1927–
AMERICAN POLITICIAN

Armstrong is best remembered for a string of significant "firsts." She was the first female cochair of the Republican National Committee. Armstrong made a dramatic move in 1974: on reviewing the published transcripts of the Watergate tapes, she resigned her post and demanded the resignation of President Richard Nixon. She was one of the first high-level Washington Republicans to call on Nixon to step down from the presidency.

GERTRUDE FRANKLIN HORN ATHERTON, 1857–1948
AMERICAN WRITER

American critics lambasted Atherton's works for their "immorality." Her heroines defied convention, spoke their minds forcefully, and exhibited unheard-of sexual independence. After her husband died from a morphine overdose, Atherton fled to New York City to write. She never remarried, but pursued a series of affairs. The nation's reviewers were horrified. Undaunted, she continued to write searing novels about American society. Her career ran for six decades; she completed fifty-six books and pioneered the fictionalized biography. In her seventies, she settled in San Francisco, where she ran a literary salon. Her last published piece was a letter nominating Eleanor Roosevelt for president.

17

JANE AUSTEN, 1775–1817
BRITISH NOVELIST

Regarded today as a major British novelist, Jane Austen in her time was not only almost unknown as a writer, but had so much difficulty finding a publisher for her early novels that she had to publish them herself. She was known by a few, including Sir Walter Scott, but her influence on later writers was not felt until Henry James rediscovered her. The daughter of a country clergyman, she lived most of her life in small villages and wrote satirical comedies about the provincial, middle-class world she knew. *Sense and Sensibility* (1811), *Pride and Prejudice* (1813), and *Emma* (1816) are three of her most important and most popular novels.

MARGARET FRANCES (PEGGY) BACON, 1895–1987

AMERICAN ARTIST

Bacon studied at the Art Students' League in New York, where she met and married Alexander Brook. She stopped painting because Brook, whom she considered a better painter, was critical of her work in "his" medium. In 1934 a Guggenheim Foundation Fellowship funded Bacon's book *Off With Their Heads!*, which skewered thirty-nine luminaries of the art world (including Georgia O'Keeffe) in Bacon's incisive drypoint illustrations. In 1940 Bacon divorced Brook and began to paint again. Her 1953 mystery novel *The Inward Eye* won her an Edgar Allan Poe Mystery Award. She lived out the rest of her life in Cape Porpoise, Maine, continuing to paint.

Sara Josephine Baker, 1873–1945

American physician

Sara Josephine Baker was a physician and a pioneering public health administrator whose work in the poor areas of New York City helped to drastically reduce infant mortality rates. The annual death count dropped by 1,200 in one of her districts in 1908, thanks to her innovative policies stressing preventive medicine and good hygiene. One of her most noteworthy achievements was apprehending "Typhoid Mary" Mallon, a cook who had infected seven families with typhoid fever. When Baker died, the *New York Times* announced that because of her work, New York had become one of the safest cities in the United States in which to be born.

EMILY GREENE BALCH, 1867–1961
AMERICAN PACIFIST

Not every person stands up for her unpopular beliefs, suffers for them, and then is vindicated with a Nobel Prize, but Emily Balch was one such person. A long-time professor of economics and political science at Wellesley College, she was fired in 1918, at age fifty-two, for her objection to America's entry into World War I. A native of Jamaica Plain, Massachusetts, she went on to help found the Women's International League for Peace and Freedom in Geneva, to work for disarmament, and to pin her hopes for world peace on the United Nations. She was a corecipient of the Nobel Peace Prize in 1946.

21

DJUNA BARNES, 1892–1982
AMERICAN WRITER

Barnes got her start reporting on British suffragists, who occasionally died in prison from the effects of forcible feeding during hunger strikes. (Rubber feeding tubes were inserted so forcefully that suffragists sometimes died from infection or from food in their lungs.) In 1920 Barnes went to Europe to conduct interviews, some of which, including those with James Joyce and Coco Chanel, were reprinted in a 1985 collection. She is best remembered for her masterpiece *Nightwood* (1936), which explores the drifting of a sexually ambiguous woman through 1920s Paris. The book is regarded as a prime example of American expatriate writing.

NATALIE CLIFFORD BARNEY, 1876–1972

AMERICAN WRITER

As a young heiress, American-born Natalie Barney made quite a splash in Paris. She had a series of affairs with women, who wrote thinly disguised accounts of her magnetism and fickleness in love, and by her early twenties Barney had become something of a legend. She was a talented writer, but she is remembered less for her writing than for the lasting relationships she cultivated over many years with other artistic celebrities in Paris, including Gertrude Stein, Colette, and Ezra Pound. Perhaps her greatest contribution was the salon she conducted in her Paris home in which she brought influential French and American writers together.

CLARA BARTON, 1821–1912

AMERICAN TEACHER, NURSE, AND FOUNDER OF THE AMERICAN RED CROSS

The achievement that Clara Barton is best remembered for—establishing the American Red Cross—came late in her long work life, when she was sixty and had worked in Europe with the International Committee of the Red Cross. Previously, Barton had served as an unpaid nurse during the Civil War and delivered first aid equipment, which she had acquired from private donations, on the battlefield. She later founded an organization that located missing soldiers, and found approximately 13,000 of them. Before the war she had been a teacher and had founded a school in Bordentown, New Jersey. She is remembered as the "Angel of the Battlefield."

FLORENCE BASCOM, 1862–1945
AMERICAN GEOLOGIST

Bascom had a string of impressive "firsts"— she was the first woman awarded a Ph.D. by Johns Hopkins, the first woman elected a fellow of the Geological Society of America, and the first woman hired by the U.S. Geological Survey as a geologist. She also established the geology department at Bryn Mawr College and oversaw it for three decades. When she arrived at Bryn Mawr in 1895, Bascom had to work out of a makeshift laboratory in a storage area, and she conducted her research while giving her popular classes and acquiring the necessary specimens and equipment. In 1906 she was made a full professor, and in 1930 served as vice president of the Geological Society of America.

MARY ELIZABETH BASS, 1876–1956

AMERICAN PHYSICIAN

Mary Elizabeth Bass grew up in Carley, Mississippi, and studied to become a physician. One of her more noteworthy achievements was founding, with five other women physicians, the New Orleans Hospital for Women and Children, which was free to all. Three years later, Bass was one of the first women faculty members at Tulane University's School of Medicine. After her retirement, she became an important chronicler of the history of women physicians in America, amassing a collection of over 290 monographs and 1,400 pictures and clippings for what is now Tulane's Elizabeth Bass Collection. She received the Elizabeth Blackwell Centennial Medal Award in 1953.

KATHARINE LEE BATES, 1859–1929
AMERICAN EDUCATOR AND WRITER

Bates, a professor of English at Wellesley College, scaled Pike's Peak in Colorado during an 1893 summer trip to the western states. She was so inspired by the dazzling view from the summit of the 14,110-foot mountain that she wrote the poem that would later be set to music as *America, the Beautiful*. "It was then and there," she wrote of her experience, "as I was looking out over the sea-like expanse of fertile country spreading away so far under those ample skies, that the opening lines of the hymn floated into my mind."

Amy Marcy Cheney Beach,
1867–1944

American Composer

A my Cheney was playing the piano on the Boston
stage by age sixteen. At eighteen, she married H. H.
A. Beach and turned to composition. In 1892 the Boston
Handel and Haydn Society performed her Mass—the first
composition by a woman the Society ever played. When
the Boston Symphony Orchestra played her Piano
Concerto, she was the featured performer. In 1910, Beach
left for a highly successful performing tour in Europe,
returning to the States in 1914. After touring and some
minor composing, she began to produce more important
works in the late 1920s. By the time of her death, she was
considered America's premier woman composer.

APHRA BEHN, 1640–1689
BRITISH NOVELIST AND DRAMATIST

The first female professional writer for the British stage, Behn was successful as a novelist and playwright. Her most famous novel, *Oroonoko, or the History of the Royal Slave* (1678), reflects her own youth in Suriname, West Indies, and is important for having introduced the "noble savage," later explored by Jean-Jacques Rousseau. Her most popular play, *The Rover* (1677), was one of fifteen pieces notable for their intrigue and bawdiness. A friend of John Dryden, she was acclaimed in the twentieth century by Virginia Woolf in *A Room of One's Own*.

GWENDOLYN B. BENNETT, 1902–1981

AMERICAN WRITER

A graduate of Columbia and Pratt Institute, Bennett wrote influential essays on the role of the African-American artist, and composed poetry that was notable for sharp contrasts and vivid sensory images. Her column "The Ebony Flute" in the journal *Opportunity,* which dealt with trends in the black literary and artistic world, chronicled the 1920s Harlem Renaissance. Her poems addressed the forgotten heritage and need for self-determination of African-Americans. Some, like "To a Dark Girl," celebrate black standards of physical beauty; others, like "Song," mourn the absence of cultural structures to support and nurture blacks. Bennett was a gifted observer during a remarkably fertile period for black writers and artists.

MARY McLEOD BETHUNE, 1875–1955

AMERICAN EDUCATOR

Bethune, the foremost black educator of her day, served as Negro Affairs Director for the National Youth Administration from 1936 to 1944. That was her official title; unofficially, she also served as leader of the "Black Cabinet," a group of African-American officials in key federal positions who advised the White House informally on a wide variety of issues. Her work proceeded along much the same lines as that of Mary Dewson, Frances Perkins, and Eleanor Roosevelt, but was, in keeping with the attitudes of the time, limited to the concerns of members of her own race.

BENAZIR BHUTTO, 1953–
PRIME MINISTER OF PAKISTAN

Benazir Bhutto was born in Karachi. She studied politics at Harvard and international law at Oxford before returning to Pakistan, where she led the then-opposition Pakistan Peoples Party during a decade of political upheaval. Arrested nine times, Bhutto spent nearly six years under detention before becoming prime minister in 1988, the first woman to head an Islamic government. Bhutto has championed democracy, education, and health reform for the poor, and has pledged to end discrimination against women. She is the author of *Foreign Policy in Perspective* and the autobiographical *Daughter of Destiny*. Bhutto won the Bruno Kreisky Award for Human Rights in 1988.

MARY ANN BICKERDYKE, 1817–1901

AMERICAN NURSE

Bickerdyke's sole aim during the Civil War was to improve the care of wounded Union soldiers. If improving the level of care meant scrubbing up after filthy, incompetent doctors, then she would scrub every surface in sight, or antagonize the hospital staff by threatening to report drunken physicians, or order someone who was wearing garments intended for the wounded to remove the clothes immediately. Bickerdyke stepped on a lot of toes, but won most of her fights. One ruffled male appealed to General Sherman to take action against her, but was disappointed by Sherman's reply: "I can do nothing for you; she outranks me."

ELIZABETH BISHOP, 1911–1979
AMERICAN POET

In 1938, Bishop settled in Florida with Louise Crane, her lover and classmate from Vassar. During the next eight years, she wrote *North and South*, which won the 1946 Houghton Mifflin Literary Fellowship. In 1951 she traveled to Rio de Janeiro, where an acquaintance from New York, Carlota, housed her when she was ill. Bishop happily remained with "Lota" in Brazil for the next fifteen years. Her second book of poetry won the 1955 Pulitzer Prize. In 1967, Lota overdosed on sedatives, and Bishop never regained her happiness. She taught at Harvard from 1970 until her death. She released *Geography III* in 1976, and died in her Boston apartment in 1979.

Isabel Bishop, 1902–1988
American painter

In the early 1930s, Bishop hit on the style that would characterize her work for the rest of her career. She became interested in the hurrying figures she saw near her studio in Manhattan; time is of the essence in Bishop's work. She is never a participant but always a loving observer—a result of her lonely childhood. Bishop married Harold Wolff in 1934 and moved to Riverdale, New York, but continued to paint. She was particularly interested in painting young working women. She was sensitive to the small, everyday preparations they made in public and private. Her very personal work is recognized as a major contribution to American art.

ANTOINETTE BROWN BLACKWELL, 1825–1921

AMERICAN MINISTER

Antoinette Brown became the first woman minister of a recognized denomination in the United States when, in 1853, she was ordained as a minister of the First Congregational Church in Butler and Savannah, Wayne County, New York. It had not been an easy achievement. Though she had graduated from Oberlin College and had done the course work at Oberlin's theological graduate school, the professors refused to give her a license to preach or to graduate her in 1850. She lectured widely in her quest to become ordained. In later years she married, had seven children, wrote several books, and lived long enough to vote in 1920.

ELIZABETH BLACKWELL, 1821–1910

AMERICAN PHYSICIAN

The British-born Blackwell decided to embark on a career as a physician when a female friend described her discomfort at being examined by a male doctor. Blackwell's plans did not meet with instant success, however: she was rejected by twenty-nine American medical schools before New York's Geneva College finally accepted her in 1847. On completing her studies and residency, she became the first female physician in the United States. She was beset by derisive publicity, but finally established a practice in New York City in 1851. Her one-room clinic eventually became the New York Infirmary for Women and Children, which is still in operation today.

BONNIE BLAIR, 1964–
AMERICAN SPEED SKATER

It was a move by her family from Cornwell, New York, to Champaign, Illinois, that turned Bonnie Blair into a speed skater. Champaign was a hotbed of speed-skating. Great coaching, rigorous training, and a positive attitude helped Blair in her ascendancy in the speed-skating world, particularly in the 500- and 1,000-meter events. Blair won Olympic gold medals in 1988 and 1992.

FLORENCE ABY BLANCHFIELD, 1882–1971

AMERICAN MILITARY NURSE

This Virginia-born army nurse spent World War I tending wounded soldiers in France, and continued to serve in the Army Nurses' Corps (ANC) all over the world after the war. Promoted to superintendent in 1943, Blanchfield worked to propel nurses into the thick of the military, training them in military regulations and assigning them to front-line positions. Her efforts helped in the passage of the 1947 Army-Navy Nurse Act, which granted nurses full status in the military. Blanchfield received the first commission ever awarded to a woman in the U.S. Army. Her many awards include the army's Distinguished Service Medal and the Florence Nightingale Medal.

AMELIA JENKS BLOOMER, 1818–1894

AMERICAN SUFFRAGIST

This self-educated reformer was born in Homer, New York. In 1849, she founded *The Lily,* a periodical devoted to topics of interest to women. For six years she used its pages to promote temperance and women's suffrage and to preach against sexual discrimination. Bloomer was also popular on the lecture circuit and became famous for her views on dress reform. At a time when women wore restrictive corsets and floor-length skirts, she appeared in public wearing loose trousers under a knee-length skirt (the trousers were eventually named "bloomers" after her). Regrettably, the comfortable and practical garments did not catch on with the general public.

NELLIE BLY, 1864–1922
AMERICAN WRITER

She was a journalist whose real name was Elizabeth Cochrane Seaman, but it was under the assumed name of Nellie Bly that she feigned insanity in order to observe and expose the inhumane conditions at the notorious Blackwell's Island women's asylum in 1887. Later, she beat the record set by "Phileas Fogg" for circling the globe in eighty days. Her *Around the World in 72 Days* described her real-life journeys by steamboat, rickshaw, railroad, and even sampan.

LOUISE BOGAN, 1897–1970

AMERICAN POET

An energetic and prolific poet and critic for over half a century, Louise Bogan survived two unhappy marriages, fought depression, and raised her daughter alone while establishing her career. Having studied at Boston University and Radcliffe, the Maine native was having her poems published in well-known magazines like *The New Republic* by 1921. Her first book, *Body of This Death*, was published in 1923 to great acclaim. Bogan was appointed to the staff of *The New Yorker* as poetry critic in 1931, and she held the Library of Congress's chair in poetry from 1945 to 1946. Bogan's memoirs were published posthumously in *The New Yorker* in 1978.

ERMA BOMBECK, 1927–1996

AMERICAN WRITER

Born Erma Fiste in Dayton, Ohio, this writer started her career working as a copy girl and reporter for the *Dayton Journal Herald* while she attended college. She married William Bombeck, a high school teacher, in 1949. Bombeck began her column in the 1960s, earning three dollars per column. The column, "At Wit's End," was a huge success, and by 1967 it was being syndicated by some 900 newspapers. Bombeck wrote about domestic themes such as housework, child rearing, and marriage, putting a unique and humorous spin on ordinary situations. Her books include *Motherhood: The Second Oldest Profession* and *Aunt Erma's Cope Book*.

ANNE BONNY, 1697?–?

IRISH-BORN PIRATE

A legendary pirate, Bonny was definitely not someone to be trifled with. When her father disinherited her in 1715, she burned down his South Carolina plantation and fled to the present-day Bahamas. As she disembarked from her ship, a one-eared sailor attempted to block her way, demanding that she have a drink with him. She drew her pistol and blasted off his other ear. The crew stared, amazed. "By God," Bonny howled, "is that a head? I thought I was shooting the handle off a mug." Bonny was the lover of Mary Read, another notorious female pirate.

EVANGELINE CORY BOOTH,
1865–1950
BRITISH-BORN SOCIAL REFORMER

Evangeline Booth's father, William Booth, left the Methodist ministry to found an independent evangelistic organization that became the Salvation Army. By the age of seventeen, Evangeline was preaching the gospel on her own, earning the moniker "White Angel of the Slums." In 1904, she began her thirty-year career as leader of the Salvation Army in the United States. Under Booth's leadership, the Army established soup kitchens, hospitals for unwed mothers, and emergency disaster relief efforts. Booth also organized canteens for World War I soldiers in France, for which she earned the Distinguished Service Medal in 1919. In 1934 she assumed leadership of the international organization, which she ran for five years.

QUEEN BOUDICCA,
FIRST CENTURY A.D.
BRITISH RULER

When the Romans demanded the repayment of funds given to Queen Boudicca's late husband, King Prasutagus, she refused. They flogged her and publicly raped her daughters. Believing they had taught her a lesson, the Romans let her live—a mistake, as she was bent on revenge. Boudicca called on the many small kingdoms on the island to unify, and butchered her way southward to London. She countenanced unspeakable atrocities against the Romans and their allies, mutilating and skewering her opponents by the hundreds. Boudicca nearly triumphed, but she fell to Roman forces despite an overwhelming numerical advantage. She and her daughters committed suicide before they could be taken by the enemy.

MARGARET BOURKE-WHITE, 1904–1971

AMERICAN PHOTOJOURNALIST

Margaret Bourke-White became a celebrity in the early days of *Life* magazine, when photojournalism brought the news to readers in a new and immediate way. *Life's* first cover story, in 1936, was one of Bourke-White's, and the magazine glamorized its courageous young photojournalist. Throughout her career, Bourke-White had a reputation for taking risks and bullying even sick or dying subjects in order to get the best shot. She explained, "These little inconveniences will be forgotten tomorrow and my pictures will live forever." Indeed, Bourke-White's photographs brought the suffering of her subjects to wider attention and, as she predicted, the photos have been celebrated long after her death.

47

MARY ELIZABETH BOWSER, 1839–?
AMERICAN UNION SPY

Even after gaining her freedom on the death of her master, John Van Lew, ex-slave Bowser remained with his Virginia family. The family sent her north to Philadelphia to get an education, but when the Civil War broke out, Bowser returned to Richmond. There Mrs. Van Lew landed her a servant's position in Jefferson Davis's Confederate White House. While pretending to be a harmless idiot, Bowser drank in all the Confederate plans she overheard, as well as obtaining access to documents. She relayed all her information back to Mrs. Van Lew, who passed it on to the Union's General Grant, thwarting many of the Confederacy's military efforts.

ANNE BRADSTREET, 1612?–1672
AMERICAN POET

Bradstreet was America's first published poet. She abandoned a life among the nobility in England to settle with her husband in Massachusetts sometime before 1644. Her poems were first published in London in 1650 in a collection entitled *The Tenth Muse Lately Sprung Up in America*. A later collection, *Several Poems Compiled with Great Variety (of) Wit and Learning*, was published posthumously. Her verses, composed while Bradstreet attended to her family of ten, offer fascinating insights on Puritan life in the colonies. They express Bradstreet's love for her husband, her anguish at the death of a child, her fear of death in childbirth, and the determination to go on in the face of hardship.

EMMA LUCY BRAUN, 1889–1971
AMERICAN ECOLOGIST

B raun used her knowledge of botany to work for the conservation of natural habitats in and around her home in Cincinnati. She earned her bachelor's degree, her master's in geology, and her Ph.D. in botany at the University of Cincinnati, where she rose from assistant in botany in 1914 to associate professor in 1927. In 1935, she became the first woman president of the Ohio Academy of Science. In 1951 she established and headed the Ohio Flora Committee under the Ohio Academy of Science. Braun also wrote many articles arguing for the conservation of wildlife habitats. She died at home at the age of eighty-one.

Margaret Brent, 1600?–1670
American Suffragist

Brent's career seems to have taken off when she was named executor of the will of the governor of Maryland. Brent later bought land and appeared frequently in court with her many male adversaries. She always represented herself, and she won every case. Brent made a landmark plea in 1647, when she argued that she should be granted two votes in the colonial assembly—one as a landowner and the other as an attorney. The ingenious request was denied, but it made Brent the first American suffragist.

LAURA BRIDGMAN, 1829–1889
AMERICAN EDUCATOR

Although Bridgman survived a scarlet fever epidemic, the disease left her blind, deaf, and mute and destroyed much of her sense of smell and taste. Between the ages of two and seven, Laura drifted beyond the world of human contact and stimulus. On hearing of her case, Dr. Samuel Gridley Howe, director of the Perkins Institute for the Blind in Watertown, Massachusetts, challenged the popular belief that people like Laura could never be taught to communicate. Within a few months, Laura could write letters; within a few years she was writing poetry, and eventually she wrote her autobiography. Bridgman later became an instructor at the Perkins Institute. Her successful case inspired Anne Sullivan, Helen Keller's "miracle worker."

Augusta Fox Bronner, 1881–1966

American psychologist

In 1901, her first year of teaching, Bronner showed an aptitude for handling difficult students. Her doctoral thesis at Columbia University's Teachers College was a ground-breaking study of delinquent and mentally deficient girls. The study became a classic, and contributed to the understanding of both delinquent behavior and the behavior of the mentally disabled. She cofounded the Judge Baker Children's Center in Boston; one of the first of its kind, it was a model for countless others in America and abroad. Bronner lectured at Boston University, Simmons College, and the FBI training school. The Center still offers outreach programs to children in the Boston area.

CHARLOTTE BRONTË, 1816–1855
BRITISH NOVELIST

Charlotte Brontë was arguably the most accomplished member of one of the most talented literary families in history. Raised strictly in a secluded part of Yorkshire, England, she and her three siblings amused themselves by writing poetry and adventure stories about fanciful lands. Charlotte, using the pseudonym Currer Bell, was the first to publish a novel. *Jane Eyre,* a haunting Gothic novel with an autobiographical component, was an immediate success when it appeared in 1847. Soon afterward, her siblings Emily, Anne, and Branwell all died within an eight-month period. Left alone to care for an ailing father, Brontë nevertheless produced two more novels, *Shirley* and *Villette*.

GWENDOLYN BROOKS, 1917–

AMERICAN POET

Brooks's vivid writing is grounded in black American life, and in the constant personal and cultural pressures in African-American communities. Her 1949 *Annie Allen*, her second collection of poems, won Brooks the 1950 Pulitzer Prize for Poetry—a first for African-Americans. Brooks continued to write prolifically, for adults as well as for children. Her later works include *Riot* (1969), *Family Pictures* (1970), and *Report from Part One: An Autobiography* (1972).

HELEN GURLEY BROWN, 1922–

AMERICAN WRITER AND MAGAZINE EDITOR

An innovative writer and editor, Brown was born in Arkansas and began her working career as a secretary. Her flair for writing earned her a promotion to copywriter at a Los Angeles advertising agency, and she rose to become one of the nation's best-paid copywriters. In 1962, Brown wrote *Sex and the Single Girl,* a bestseller that was subsequently translated into sixteen languages. The success of the book gained Brown the position of editor at *Cosmopolitan* magazine. She transformed it from a staid and unsuccessful publication into a lively and popular single woman's guide to careers, sex, and adventure. Brown was awarded the Henry Johnson Fisher Award in 1996.

ELIZABETH BARRETT BROWNING, 1806–1861

BRITISH POET

Remembered mostly for her book of love poems, *Sonnets from the Portuguese*, Barrett Browning was an important and popular poet in England before her future husband, Robert, came into the picture in 1845. Though she was raised in genteel comfort, a riding accident at age fifteen left her an invalid. Her mother died soon thereafter, and her father suffered severe financial setbacks, both of which contributed to her ill health. She eloped with Robert in 1846 and they moved to Florence, where her health improved and where their mutual love and respect nurtured the work of both.

PEARL S. BUCK, 1892–1973
AMERICAN WRITER

Born in Hillsboro, West Virginia, Pearl Sydenstryker was brought to China at an early age by her missionary parents. She grew up bilingual and was greatly influenced by Chinese literature. In 1917, she married agriculture expert John Lossing Buck. Through his work, she became familiar with life on a Chinese farm, and this would later be the setting of some of her best fiction. In 1938, she was awarded the Nobel Prize. Buck used her prominent position to back causes dear to her, and increasingly her fiction incorporated her views. In later years, the Pearl S. Buck Foundation set up centers to aid children in several countries. Buck continued to write at the rate of nearly a book a year until her death at the age of eighty-one.

EMMA BUGBEE, 1888–1981

AMERICAN JOURNALIST

Born in Shippensburg, Pennsylvania, Bugbee attended Barnard College in New York, where she was a campus correspondent for the *New York Herald Tribune*. After Bugbee graduated, the paper hired her for a full-time position, but as a woman at the *Tribune*, she was a second-class citizen. By 1914, she finally won her byline and a desk in the city room. Like her friend Eleanor Roosevelt, Bugbee encouraged women reporters. Her five-book "Peggy" series, starting with the classic *Peggy Covers the News* (1936), inspired many young readers. Until her retirement in 1966, four years after Eleanor Roosevelt's death, she was a welcoming presence for younger women reporters at the *Tribune*.

Martha Cannary Burk (Calamity Jane), 1852?–1903

American Frontierswoman

While there is no doubt that a rough-and-tumble but sympathetic frontierswoman known as Calamity Jane existed, her real life story is a mystery. The legend of Calamity Jane evolved through frontier folklore, the Wild West shows she performed in, and popular, idealistic fiction. Jane herself was apparently a hard-drinking prostitute who traveled from man to man, sometimes dressed as a man, and sometimes worked at jobs men normally held. Her most famous liaison was with Wild Bill Hickok. Her nickname derives possibly from her ability to shoot a pistol when drunk, possibly from her willingness to nurse the troubled and sick, or possibly from both.

60

LUCY BURNS, 1879–1966
AMERICAN SUFFRAGIST

Together with legendary activist Alice Paul, Burns organized a massive women's suffrage parade on March 3, 1913, in Washington, D.C. It was probably no coincidence that that was also the date on which Woodrow Wilson was to be inaugurated as president of the United States. When Wilson showed up at the Capitol, he found that his greeters had left to see the parade. The column of over five thousand marchers demanding a constitutional amendment granting women the right to vote made quite a splash as they elbowed their way down crowded Pennsylvania Avenue. The amendment they sought was passed and ratified before Wilson left office.

ADA AUGUSTA BYRON
(LADY LOVELACE), 1815–1852
BRITISH MATHEMATICIAN

E ven though she lived in an era of looms and spindles rather than semiconductors, it is no coincidence that Ada's name is also that of a computer language used by the U.S. Department of Defense. Her natural talent for mathematics led her to make valuable contributions to the first, punchcard-activated "computers" developed for the textile industry in the 1830s by Charles Babbage. For her part, Ada is generally regarded as the first computer programmer in history.

MARY STEICHEN CALDERONE, 1904–1998

AMERICAN EDUCATOR

Physician and educator Mary Calderone earned her medical degree from the University of Rochester and her master's degree in public health from Columbia University. She served as medical director for Planned Parenthood for over a decade, then cofounded and became president of the Sex Information and Education Council of the United States. Throughout her career she fought to introduce sex education into American public schools. Calderone's publications include *Sexuality and Human Values* and *Talking with Your Child About Sex*. Her many awards have included the Elizabeth Blackwell Award for Distinguished Services to Humanity, as well as twelve honorary degrees.

MARIA CALLAS, 1923–1977
AMERICAN DIVA

The acclaimed soprano Maria Callas launched her professional career with her starring appearance in *La Gioconda* at the Arena Verona. The New York native was known for taking on notoriously difficult roles such as Brunhilde, Turandot, and Isolde, earning her admiration and respect. Despite her success, Callas battled insecurity and weight problems all her life. "Only when I was singing did I feel loved," she reflected. Callas's later career was marked by her deteriorating voice and her disastrous affair with Aristotle Onassis, for whom she broke off her marriage to her manager, Giovanni Battista Meneghini. Callas left the opera stage in 1965, but continued to sing in recitals until her death.

ANNIE JUMP CANNON, 1863–1941
AMERICAN ASTRONOMER

A nnie Cannon was the daughter of Wilson and Mary Cannon, a Delaware state senator and an amateur astronomer. She earned her master's degree in astronomy from Wellesley College in 1907. After Wellesley, she moved on to Harvard. In 1918, Cannon undertook, along with fellow astronomer Edward Pickering, a project to classify 350,000 different stars. She completed the project on her own after Pickering's death. Cannon was made an honorary member of the Royal Astronomical Society in 1914, and her other honors include the National Academy of Sciences' Draper Medal and an honorary degree from Oxford.

HATTIE WYATT CARAWAY, 1878–1950

UNITED STATES SENATOR

Hattie Wyatt was born in rural Tennessee and married lawyer Thaddeus Caraway. She raised two children while her husband entered local politics and worked his way up to become a U.S. senator from Arkansas in 1920. After his 1931 death, Hattie was appointed to serve out her husband's second term while a successor was chosen. However, Louisiana senator Huey Long persuaded her to campaign for re-election, and in 1932 she became the first woman to be elected to the U.S. Senate in her own right. Caraway was a staunch supporter of Roosevelt's New Deal. In 1943 she cosponsored an early version of the Equal Rights Amendment.

EMILY CARR, 1871–1945
CANADIAN ARTIST

Carr left British Columbia to study art in San Francisco and London. In 1902, she had a physical and mental breakdown, and recovered at a sanatorium in the English countryside. She spent the next six years in Vancouver, painting and teaching. In 1910, Carr moved to Paris to continue her work, but unfortunately, the hard work renewed her "hysterical" symptoms. She eventually fought off her illness to produce the first of her abstract paintings. Back in Canada, Carr won recognition with her dramatic Canadian landscapes. But even as she mastered her art and gained recognition, she developed heart trouble. She took up writing, and wrote autobiographically for nearly ten years.

RACHEL CARSON, 1907–1964
AMERICAN ENVIRONMENTALIST

Rachel Carson is best known as the author of *Silent Spring*, an urgent warning about the poisons pumped into our water, soil, and atmosphere by industry and agriculture. She earned a master's degree in zoology from Johns Hopkins and went on to become a junior aquatic biologist at the United States Bureau of Fisheries in Washington, D.C., writing in her free time. The success of her book *The Sea Around Us* (1951) made it possible for her to devote herself to writing full time. *Silent Spring*, published in 1960, gave birth to the modern environmental movement and inspired governmental measures to curb the use of DDT and other wildlife-killing chemicals.

MARY SHADD CARY, 1823–1893
AMERICAN EDITOR

Born a free woman in Delaware in 1823, Cary had to travel to Pennsylvania for her education, since her home state refused to offer blacks schooling of any kind. Cary, the first African-American woman to edit a newspaper, founded the *Provincial Freeman* in 1853. Her readers were fugitive slaves who had crossed the border into Canada. Cary eventually earned a law degree from Howard University.

MARY CASSATT, 1844–1926
AMERICAN PAINTER

One of the first American artists—and perhaps the first woman artist—to live and work as an expatriate in Europe, Mary Cassatt achieved singular fame as an impressionist painter in France. Born in Allegheny City, Pennsylvania, she studied at the Pennsylvania Academy of Fine Arts in Philadelphia. After moving to France in 1866, she attracted the attention of Edgar Degas, who influenced her, and she was the only American to exhibit with the French impressionists. She became primarily a figure painter, concentrating on the mother and child theme. Her career slowed in 1912 when cataracts were removed from both eyes, and it ended five years later when she became blind.

Willa Cather, 1873–1947
American writer

Cather was born near Gore, Virginia. In 1896, after graduating from college, she moved to Pittsburgh, where she edited and wrote for local magazines and newspapers. Her first break came when she published a story collection, *The Troll Garden* (1905). In 1906 Cather moved to New York, where she became managing editor of *McClure's* magazine. After her first novel, *Alexander's Bridge* (1912), was serialized in *McClure's*, she left the magazine to write full time. Cather was assured of her status as a writer when she won the Pulitzer Prize. She often retreated to Jaffrey, New Hampshire, to write undisturbed. When Cather died in 1947, her last wishes—that her novel-in-progress be destroyed, and that she be buried in Jaffrey—were carried out.

CATHERINE THE GREAT, 1729–1796

EMPRESS OF RUSSIA

This daughter of a minor German prince married Grand Duke Peter, heir to the Russian throne. Peter assumed the throne in 1761; erratic and unstable, he was deposed and murdered by the Imperial Guards a year later. Catherine became the absolute monarch of the largest empire in Europe, and it grew even larger during her thirty-four-year reign. She hoped to use the ideas of the Enlightenment to complete the process of westernization begun by Peter I. Catherine established the first Russian schools for girls and promoted improvements in agriculture and health care. Unfortunately, the average Russian became worse off as the institution of serfdom was strengthened under her rule.

CARRIE CHAPMAN CATT, 1859–1947

AMERICAN SUFFRAGIST

Catt is best remembered for her tireless commitment to winning the vote for women. Born in Ripon, Wisconsin, she taught for a time, then became a strong voice for the women's suffrage movement. Catt had the remarkable distinction of heading the National American Woman Association, as well as cofounding the National League of Women Voters. She was also an active advocate for international peace, serving as head of the National Committee on the Cause and Cure of War.

FLORENCE CHADWICK, 1918–

AMERICAN ATHLETE

Swimmer Florence Chadwick was born in San Diego and won her first race there at age eleven. Specializing in long-distance swimming, she raced for the next nineteen years. Along the way, she appeared in the 1945 film *Bathing Beauty* with former teammate Esther Williams. At age thirty, Chadwick began training to swim the English Channel. In 1950 she swam from Cape Gris-Nez, France, to Dover, England, in 13 hours, 23 minutes, breaking a twenty-four-year-old record held by Englishwoman Gertrude Ederle. Chadwick swam the Channel twice more before her retirement from the sport. In 1970, she was inducted into the International Swimming Hall of Fame.

Coco Chanel, 1883–1971

French Couturier

Gabrielle Bonheur Chanel is the most imitated fashion designer in history. Her designs were harshly simple; to balance the design's simplicity, her fabrics were rich and luxurious, at once youthful and sophisticated. Having gotten her start in 1909 with hats, she expanded her designs to clothing five years later. The approach of World War II forced her to close her business in 1939, but she re-established herself in 1954, defying the popular romantic look of the time with spare-looking suits that became all the rage in the fashion world. A shrewd businesswoman as well as a brilliant couturier, Chanel is best known for her perfumes, particularly Chanel No. 5.

JULIA CHILD, 1912–
AMERICAN CHEF AND TELEVISION PERSONALITY

C hild revolutionized the way Americans cook by introducing the nation to French cuisine via her popular cooking show, *The French Chef,* and a book she coauthored, *Mastering the Art of French Cooking.* Child was born Julia McWilliams in Pasadena, California, and graduated from Smith College. She met her future husband, Paul Child, while serving in the OSS during World War II. The Childs moved to France in 1948, where Julia discovered her true vocation and enrolled in the Cordon Bleu cooking school. Child made her television debut in 1961, and enthusiastic audiences bolstered a long-lasting career. Her many cookbooks include *The Way to Cook* (1989).

SHIRLEY ANITA SAINT HILL CHISHOLM, 1924–

AMERICAN POLITICIAN

In 1968, as the Democratic representative of the Twelfth Congressional District of Brooklyn, Chisholm became the first African-American woman elected to Congress. She held her post for seven consecutive terms, until her retirement in 1983. She was best known as a champion of women's and minority rights, making her mark by sponsoring legislation that extended the federal minimum-wage law to cover domestic workers. After Chisholm retired from Congress, she taught at Mount Holyoke College.

KATE CHOPIN, 1851–1904
AMERICAN WRITER

Kate Chopin was born in St. Louis, Missouri, and educated in a convent school. She was widowed at the age of thirty-one and began writing shortly afterward. Her first effort was *Bayou Folk,* short stories about the Creoles and Cajuns of Louisiana. She later wrote three novels, including *The Awakening* (1899). The novel was criticized at the time of its publication for its "themes of infidelity and passion," and Chopin gave up writing as a result. Half a century later, the work was finally recognized as a brilliant portrait of a woman whose needs for sexual and artistic fulfillment were at odds with her conventional marriage.

AGATHA CHRISTIE, 1891–1976
BRITISH NOVELIST AND PLAYWRIGHT

Agatha Christie did not become a household name until 1926, when she published her sixth novel, *The Murder of Roger Ackroyd*—a book that not only featured her unconventional sleuth, Hercule Poirot, but revolutionized plot structure in detective fiction. Born in Torquay, the rural English county that is the setting for many of her mysteries, she traveled all her life, mostly to the Middle East—the other setting she is known for. In addition to Poirot, she created Miss Jane Marple, who solved murders in novels such as *What Mrs. McGillcuddy Saw!* She also wrote plays, including *The Mousetrap* and *Witness for the Prosecution*.

CONCHITA CINTRON, 1922–
PERUVIAN BULLFIGHTER

Cintron, the first female to compete at a high professional level as a bullfighter, mastered over 1,200 bulls during her career—a career that began in Lima, Peru, when she was only twelve years old. Perhaps her most triumphant moment came in Spain in 1949. She entered the ring on horseback (against the rules), dismounted, executed a textbook-perfect set of maneuvers, and tossed her sword to the ground, refusing to kill the bull, as was customary. The authorities were outraged and had her placed under arrest. The crowd cheered so loudly in her favor, however, that she was pardoned for the "transgression." She never appeared in the ring again.

MINNA WRIGHT CITRON, 1896–1991
AMERICAN ARTIST

At age thirty-eight, Citron divorced her husband, packed up her children, and moved to Union Square in Manhattan. A year later, she had her first solo exhibit—at the Midtown Galleries Cooperative, where she showcased her satirical skills. *Feminanities* was a series of paintings that skewered the stereotypical female; she said she wanted to "hold a mirror to the unlovely facets of a woman's mind." Citron taught for the Federal Art Project until 1937. Beginning in 1942, she worked with artists who had been transplanted from Paris during World War II, including Marc Chagall, who inspired her to turn to abstract painting. Her painting is a testament to her courage and persistence.

EDITH CLARKE, 1883–1959
AMERICAN ENGINEER

Maryland-born Clarke was the first member of the Society of Women Engineers and the first American woman to teach engineering at the college level. She began as a math and physics instructor and was eventually accepted at MIT to study electrical engineering. While at MIT, she developed "Clarke components," which streamlined many complex equations in the precomputer age. However, although Clarke received a master's degree in electrical engineering from MIT—the first woman to do so—she was initially unable to find a position as an engineer. Clarke published in 1943 what became the major textbook in her field, *Circuit Analysis of AC Power Systems, Symmetrical and Related Components*.

HILLARY RODHAM CLINTON, 1947–

AMERICAN FIRST LADY, LAWYER, AND CHILDREN'S ADVOCATE

Hillary Rodham was born in Chicago and graduated from Wellesley College with honors. At Yale Law School she edited the *Yale Review* and met her future husband, Bill Clinton. In 1973, she became a staff attorney for the Children's Defense Fund, and in 1975 she moved to Arkansas, where she and Clinton were married. Rodham Clinton became a partner with a Little Rock law firm and continued her career through her husband's ascendance to the Arkansas governor's seat and then to the U.S. presidency. She has been a tireless advocate for bettering the lives of children through political action. Her most recent achievement is the bestseller *It Takes a Village and Other Lessons Children Teach Us.*

Jacqueline Cochran, 1912–1980

American Pilot

Beginning in the 1930s and continuing until 1965, Cochran was a competitor in a dizzying number of international air races; she won the prestigious Bendix transcontinental race in 1934 and later became the first woman to break the sound barrier. Cochran was one of the creators of the Women's Air Service Pilots (WASP) group during World War II. She was elected to the U.S. Aviation Hall of Fame in 1971.

CATHERINE COFFIN,
DATES UNKNOWN

AMERICAN ABOLITIONIST

Together with her husband Levi, Catherine worked as an early "conductor" on the historic Underground Railroad made famous by the legendary Harriet Tubman. The "railroad" helped slaves escape from the South through a series of clandestine hiding-stations in abolitionist households. Devout Quakers, the Coffins had the distinction of aiding the escape of a slave girl named Eliza, who was later immortalized as the heroine of Harriet Beecher Stowe's *Uncle Tom's Cabin*. (The Coffins appeared in the book as well, though their names were changed to Halliday.) The Coffins helped more than 3,000 slaves cross the border to freedom in Canada.

THERESE COINCOIN, 1742–1816
EX-SLAVE TURNED PLANTATION OWNER

This former slave was the long-time concubine of a Frenchman named Claude Metoyer, who purchased her freedom for her. When the two parted—apparently amicably—in 1786, he deeded her a large expanse of prime Louisiana land. Coincoin took to agricultural life with a vengeance, raising corn, cotton, and tobacco and managing cattle as well. The estate was quite profitable, and enabled her to purchase the freedom of her children and leave them a substantial inheritance.

Sidonie Gabrielle Colette, 1873–1954

French Writer

This acclaimed writer is known for her insights into human nature and her ability to convey vivid, sensual images in her writing. Colette led a colorful and unconventional life, with three husbands, numerous lovers, and stints as an actress, journalist, and music-hall mime. Her first husband appropriated her first literary efforts, publishing them under his own name, but after their divorce she won fame on her own. *Cheri,* published in 1920, chronicles a youth's love affair with an aging courtesan. Colette's novella *Gigi* was later made into a highly successful American film. She was one of the few Frenchwomen to be honored with membership in the Legion of Honor.

Janet Collins, 1923–
American dancer

As a young African-American dancer, Janet Collins made a choice that could have ended her career before it began. Collins was offered a position with the prestigious Ballet Russe de Monte Carlo; the offer required Collins to wear white makeup to hide her dark skin. She bluntly refused and walked away from the opportunity. Collins went on to a successful career both as a soloist and as a member of the Katherine Dunham ensemble. She eventually became the prima ballerina for the New York Metropolitan Opera.

NADIA COMANECI, 1961–
ROMANIAN GYMNAST

This athlete captivated audiences at the 1976 Montreal Olympic Games when she was just fourteen years old. Born in Onesti, Romania, Comaneci was recruited by gymnastics coach Bela Karolyi at the age of six. At the 1976 Olympics, she won perfect scores (the first ever) and three gold medals for her performances on the balance beam, the uneven parallel bars, and the all-around event. She also carried away a silver and a bronze. The Associated Press acclaimed her as Female Athlete of the Year. In 1989, Comaneci made a daring escape from Romania to Hungary, and she subsequently defected to the United States.

CHARLOTTE CORDAY, 1768–1793
FRENCH REVOLUTIONARY

Corday was born in Saint-Saturnin, France, and educated in a convent school. A devotee of the ideals of the Enlightenment, she favored social reform but believed that reform was possible within the confines of the existing monarchy. After the French Revolution broke out in 1789, she sympathized with the moderate Girondists rather than with radicals such as Marat and Robespierre, who advocated violence. Corday arranged to meet with Marat on the pretext of offering him information and then stabbed him to death in his bath. During her trial, she proudly declared that she had acted alone. She was guillotined in 1793 at the age of twenty-five.

GERTY THERESA RADNITZ CORI, 1896–1957

CZECH-BORN SCIENTIST AND NOBEL PRIZE WINNER

G erty Radnitz was born in Prague. She earned her degree in medicine in 1920 and began a lifelong collaboration with her husband, Carl Cori. The pair became naturalized U.S. citizens in 1928 and moved to St. Louis in 1931 to conduct research on normal carbohydrate metabolism. They were able to synthesize glycogen in a test tube for the first time in 1939. This made it possible for her to clarify the workings of childhood glycogen storage diseases, showing that a hereditary disease could stem from a defect in an enzyme. In 1947, Gerty Cori and her husband Carl won the Nobel Prize in medicine and physiology as a pair.

MAIREAD CORRIGAN, 1944–, AND BETTY WILLIAMS, 1943–

IRISH PEACE ACTIVISTS

In 1976, Mairead Corrigan and Betty Williams won the Nobel Peace Prize for their efforts to bring peace to Northern Ireland. Both were born in Belfast and raised as Catholics. Corrigan was active in local charity organizations. In 1976, three of Corrigan's nieces and nephews were killed, and her sister injured, in an episode of sectarian street violence. With thousands of Belfast residents protesting the violence, Corrigan and Williams cofounded Community of Peace People. Williams expressed the group's aims in her famous lecture: "We are for life and creation, and we are against war and destruction, and . . . we screamed that the violence had to stop."

ELISABETH MAY ADAMS CRAIG, 1888–1975

AMERICAN JOURNALIST

One of the first women to cover the White House, Craig once surprised John F. Kennedy by asking what he had done for women lately. "Obviously, Mrs. Craig," he said with a smile, "not enough." Craig had her own byline by 1931, and in 1943 she headed the Women's National Press Club. She pressed for the inclusion of a women's rights clause in the Civil Rights Act of 1964. Craig was a fearless foreign correspondent who worked at the front lines during World War II and the Korean War. She spent time on a combat ship at sea, in a plane over the North Pole, and in England during World War II bombing raids.

PRUDENCE CRANDALL, 1803–1890
AMERICAN EDUCATOR

C randall was head of a female boarding school in Canterbury, Connecticut, that operated quietly and with little notice until 1833, when a young black girl named Sarah Harris applied for admission. Crandall's decision to admit her set off a firestorm of controversy that resulted in mob attacks, the physical relocation of the class sites, and, eventually, Crandall's own imprisonment. The conflict was the turning point in the quiet Quaker woman's career; she decided to limit admission solely to young black women thereafter, and vowed to work for "the remaining part of my life to benefit the people of color."

IMOGEN CUNNINGHAM, 1883–1976
AMERICAN PHOTOGRAPHER

Born in Portland, Oregon, Cunningham opened a portrait studio in Seattle in 1910. Her portraits were soft-focus, but had a straightforwardness that carried over into her later work. She had refined her style to new levels by 1920, and with Ansel Adams was a founding member of the "f/64" group, who rejected the soft focus of pre-World War II photography in favor of crisp focus. Cunningham was known for her portraits of prominent contemporaries, including Gertrude Stein and Herbert Hoover. In 1967, Cunningham was one of two women elected to fellowship in the National Academy of Arts and Sciences. Cunningham's work has been much honored and has been exhibited on both coasts.

MARIE CURIE, 1867–1934

POLISH-BORN PHYSICIST AND NOBEL PRIZE WINNER

Marie Curie was born Manya Sklodowska in Warsaw, Poland. She traveled to Paris to study mathematics and physics at the Sorbonne, where she met her future husband, Pierre Curie, another accomplished scientist. While studying the properties of pitchblende, a radioactive ore, Marie theorized that it contained an undiscovered radioactive element. The Curies collaborated to isolate that element, which they named radium, and another new element, polonium. In 1903, they received the Nobel Prize for Physics. After Pierre's sudden death, Curie became the first female lecturer at the Sorbonne, and the first person to win a second Nobel Prize, for her work in chemistry.

Lydia Barrington Darragh, 1729–1789

American Spy

The British who occupied Lydia Darragh's home in Philadelphia on the night of December 2, 1777 during the Revolutionary War did not anticipate that she would listen at the keyhole, memorize the details of their forthcoming plan of attack against Washington's army, and then (under the pretext of buying flour at an out-of-town mill) speed to the American general's position at Whitemarsh to alert him. This she did, and when the British launched their attack they found Washington and his men ready. Without the intelligence it received from Mrs. Darragh, the Continental army, instead of forcing the British troops to return to Philadelphia, would almost certainly have been decimated.

DOROTHY DAY, 1897–1980
FOUNDER OF THE AMERICAN CATHOLIC WORKER MOVEMENT

Dorothy Day was thirty-five years old when she found a way to join her two passions, radical socialist activism and religious faith, by starting a newspaper in New York, *The Catholic Worker*. Her goal was nothing less than a transformation of society, particularly its class structure and its penchant for armed aggression. While she had great success with the newspaper and later with a national movement, rooted in the paper's ideals, that provided shelter for the homeless, she encountered continuing trouble over her pacifist convictions. She wrote two books—*The Eleventh Virgin*, a novel about abortion, and *The Long Loneliness*, an autobiography.

SIMONE DE BEAUVOIR, 1908–1986
FRENCH EXISTENTIALIST AND FEMINIST

De Beauvoir left a vast intellectual legacy of feminist and literary contributions. A leader of the French existentialist movement, she earned her degree in philosophy from the Sorbonne in 1929. Best known for her non-fictional *The Second Sex* (1949), she also wrote a great deal of fiction, including *She Came to Stay* (1943) and *The Mandarins* (1954), a fictionalized portrayal of Jean-Paul Sartre's existentialist clan. *The Second Sex* is a groundbreaking treatise on women's second-class-citizen role in society. Among de Beauvoir's autobiographical works is *The Coming of Age* (1970), in which she explores the approaches of various cultures to old age and comes to terms with her own aging process.

Carolina Maria de Jesus, dates unknown
Brazilian Writer

C arolina's mother insisted she go to school to learn to read and write. As an adult, Carolina settled in São Paulo's slums, where she raised three children alone. As an escape from her oppressive lifestyle, de Jesus wrote poems, plays, and stories on a broad range of topics. She also kept a diary about life in the slums, blaming Brazilian politicians for the country's severe economic inequality. One day, her writing was discovered by a reporter who requested permission to publish her work. De Jesus's career was launched. Her diary was eventually published in book form; it became the best-selling title in Brazilian history.

MARY DENNETT, 1872–1947
AMERICAN EDUCATOR AND ACTIVIST

A pioneer in the early movement for women's reproductive rights, in 1915 Dennett founded the National Birth Control League, the first organization in the country to lobby for liberalization of birth control laws. Dennett was also an early challenger of obscenity laws. When her articles on sex education were deemed obscene by the courts in 1922, she continued to distribute them anyway, incurring hefty fines in the process. Her conviction was later overturned.

MAYA DEREN, 1917–1961
AMERICAN FILMMAKER

A year after her graduation from Smith College, Deren began working with African-American dancer and choreographer Katherine Dunham, whose Caribbean-inspired dances struck a chord in Deren. Deren's repertory of artistic tools grew with her marriage to a Czechoslovakian cinematographer, Alexander Hammid. He taught her, in her own words, "the mechanics of film expression and . . . the principle of infinite pains." They coproduced *Meshes of the Afternoon*, her best-known film. By 1946, she was one of the leading lights of experimental film. Less than a year later, she became the first woman *and* the first American to win the Cannes Grand Prix Internationale for Avant-Garde Film for her first four films.

GLADYS ROWENA HENRY DICK, 1881–1963

AMERICAN PHYSICIAN

Gladys Henry earned her M.D. from Johns Hopkins. At the University of Chicago, she met and married George Dick; they worked for nearly ten years identifying the bacteria that caused scarlet fever. In 1923 they identified hemolytic streptococci. Within a year they developed a skin test; the "Dick test" was immediately usable worldwide, and the team began developing an antiserum. They patented their methods of producing the toxin and antitoxin, and thereby started a controversy—opponents argued that the patents would block further research and biological standardization. The Dicks won in court, but the question became moot in the 1940s with the development of antibiotics.

EMILY DICKINSON, 1830–1886
AMERICAN POET

Accomplished poet Emily Dickinson was born into a prominent family in Amherst, Massachusetts. She studied for a year at nearby Mount Holyoke, but was distressed by the religious fervor she found there and returned home. After what some say may have been a failed romance, Dickinson began writing poems, which are characterized by their unusual rhymes and syntax and by their emotional intensity and honesty. Fearing she would be misunderstood, Dickinson did not attempt to publish her work. She continued to live a reclusive life at home and poured out her inner life in her poems, which numbered in the hundreds by the time of her death.

MARLENE DIETRICH, 1901–1992
GERMAN-BORN ACTRESS

Marlene Dietrich began her career as a stage actress in Berlin and rocketed to fame when director Josef von Sternberg cast her as a femme fatale in the critically acclaimed film *The Blue Angel* in 1930. In the early thirties she starred in a series of films in Hollywood. When World War II broke out, she resisted Hitler's efforts to convince her to return to Germany and instead sided with the Allies, working for anti-Nazi causes, selling war bonds, and entertaining the troops. She ultimately made thirty-five films in Hollywood, including *A Foreign Affair* and *Witness for the Prosecution*. When her film career came to a close, Dietrich started a successful second career as a nightclub singer.

DOROTHEA DIX, 1802–1887
AMERICAN EDUCATOR AND SOCIAL REFORMER

D ix's devotion to the institutional care of the mentally ill stemmed from her background as a teacher. Before beginning her crusade to improve the level of treatment in mental institutions, she had founded and taught at schools in Massachusetts. When she taught a Sunday school class in a Cambridge jail, the inhumane practice of imprisoning the mentally ill with criminals galvanized her to tour jails across Massachusetts, and she revealed her findings in an embarrassing public report. Mental hospital facilities in Canada and the United States were expanded and improved as a result of her efforts.

HESSIE DONAHUE,
DATES UNKNOWN
AMERICAN ENTERTAINER

A good bet to propose to any boxing fan is the
following: "True or false—the first person ever to
knock out John L. Sullivan in a boxing ring was a woman."
You'll probably win the bet. As part of a vaudeville act,
Mrs. Hessie Donahue used to don a loose blouse,
bloomers, and boxing gloves and stand in for a few fake
rounds with the champ. One night in 1892, however,
Sullivan connected with a genuine blow to Hessie's face—
and got her mad. She retaliated with a solid punch of her
own and knocked out the previously undefeated Sullivan
for over a minute.

H. D. (Hilda Doolittle), 1886–1961

American Poet

After flunking English at Bryn Mawr College, Doolittle traveled to Europe in 1911, and she never really came home. *Sea Garden*, her first collection of poems, was published in 1916. She became the standard-bearer of the Imagists, whose poems strove for utmost clarity, and she began a lifelong affair with Annie Ellerman. In the 1930s, however, H. D. found that early fame was difficult to live up to. She wrote *Trilogy* at a fragile time in her life, and suffered a nervous breakdown. She moved to a sanitorium in Switzerland, where Ellerman paid for her treatment. Fifteen years there nurtured her next surge of creativity. H. D. died in a Zurich hospital at the age of seventy-five.

RHETA LOUISE CHILDE DORR, 1872–1948

AMERICAN JOURNALIST

Born in Omaha, Nebraska, she moved to New York City at twenty-three and joined the Art Students' League. She married John Dorr, but the marriage broke up over her continued activism and feminism. She reported on striking women workers in 1898 in a series of articles for *Hampton's* magazine. Her first book, *What Eight Million Women Want*, was a collection of those articles. During World War I, she was a foreign correspondent; her book *Inside the Russian Revolution* was published in 1917. Back in America, Dorr wrote *A Woman of Fifty* and *Susan B. Anthony: The Woman Who Changed the Mind of a Nation*.

ALICE DUNBAR-NELSON, 1875–1935

AMERICAN WRITER

A lice Ruth Moore's first book, *Violets and Other Tales* (1895), was privately printed when she was twenty. After she married the poet Paul Lawrence Dunbar, she wrote *The Goodness of St. Roque and Other Stories* (1899). After her husband's death, she relocated to Wilmington, Delaware, where she wrote a regular column on race issues for the *Washington Eagle* and edited anthologies like *Masterpieces of Negro Eloquence* (1914) and *The Dunbar Speaker and Entertainer* (1920). She remarried in 1916, and was the executive secretary of the Quaker-supported American Interracial Peace Committee from 1928 to 1931.

ISADORA DUNCAN, 1878–1927
AMERICAN DANCER

I sadora Duncan, America's first modern dancer, developed a following all over Europe that she never achieved in her native United States. Despite her popularity, she endured a series of tragedies in her personal life, including the deaths of her three children and countless failed relationships. Even as her popularity waned, she maintained her scandalous, flamboyant image with overdone hair dye and makeup, and wrote a candid autobiography, *My Life*, in 1926. In 1927, she was killed instantly when her long red scarf caught in the wheel of a sports car and broke her neck. Her funeral in Paris was attended by more than ten thousand mourners.

ETHEL COLLINS DUNHAM, 1883-1969

AMERICAN PHYSICIAN

A trailblazing pediatrician specializing in the care and treatment of premature infants, Dunham set the standard for care in this field. (As late as 1935, most hospitals had treated premature babies no differently from other newborns.) Her 1948 book *Premature Infants: A Manual for Physicians* was a landmark effort. Dunham was the first researcher to isolate prematurity as the single factor most likely to lead to infant death. In 1957, Dr. Dunham was awarded the Howland Medal, the American Pediatric Society's highest honor.

HANNAH DUSTON, 1657–1736?
AMERICAN SETTLER

When Abnakis Indians raided Haverhill, Massachusetts, and murdered Hannah Duston's week-old baby, they made a serious mistake. They took Duston and nurse Mary Neff to a New Hampshire island and told them to prepare to be stripped naked and whipped. There, however, the women encountered another hostage, a boy named Samuel Lennardson. Under cover of night, Lennardson and Duston stole some hatchets and killed all ten of their captors. Duston was responsible for nine of the fatalities. The three escaped by boat, but Hannah decided to turn back to collect the scalps of the tribesmen. Her proof of the encounter won her a hefty cash reward from the General Court in Boston.

MABEL DWIGHT, 1876–1955
AMERICAN ARTIST

Mabel Dwight is best known for her darkly funny drawings depicting city life. A classic example of her lithography is her 1936 *Queer Fish*. In an indoor aquarium, a roundish bald man with popping eyes and a downturned mouth stares at a grouper, who stares back with the same expression—one of horror. The Federal Art Project sponsored Dwight from 1935 to 1939. During this period, her work was exhibited at New York's Weyhe Gallery. Dwight wrote a famous essay, "Satire in Art," for the Project. Dwight captured the poignancies of urban life with her empathy, quiet style, and eye for humor.

AMELIA EARHART, 1898–1937
AMERICAN AVIATOR

The first woman to fly solo across the Atlantic Ocean was born in Atchison, Kansas, and attended Columbia University. After becoming the first woman to cross the Atlantic by air in 1928 (as a passenger), she decided to do the piloting herself. In 1932 she made her acclaimed transatlantic solo flight, breaking the existing time record for the crossing by completing it in 13 hours and 30 minutes. In 1937 Earhart began her first around-the-world flight with navigator Frederick Noonan. The plane vanished, and an exhaustive search by the U.S. Navy found no trace of Earhart or Noonan. Their fate remains unknown to this day.

ELIZABETH ECKFORD, 1942–
AMERICAN ACTIVIST

Together with her friend Minnie Jean Brown, fifteen-year-old Elizabeth Eckford faced down the segregationist Arkansas state government—not to mention violent mobs and hostile schoolmates—in seeking admission to Little Rock High School in 1957. The girls were two of the nine brave black students around whom the first great national crisis of the civil rights movement swirled. Federal troops were called in by the Eisenhower administration to protect them.

MARY BAKER EDDY, 1821–1910
AMERICAN RELIGIOUS LEADER

Believing herself to have been healed of her own injuries in 1866 while reading about Christ's healings in the New Testament, Eddy founded the religion now known as Christian Science—a faith based on the belief that illness is mental rather than physical. She wrote *Science and Health with Key to the Scriptures*, the Christian Science textbook, in 1875. It is now published around the world, as are many of her other writings. In 1908, she established the newspaper *The Christian Science Monitor*. In addition to Mother Teresa, she is considered one of the leading female religious figures of modern times.

GERTRUDE CAROLINE EDERLE, 1906–

AMERICAN ATHLETE

In 1926, the New York-born Ederle became the first woman to swim the English Channel. Having competed since her early teens, Ederle had many athletic awards to her credit, including setting numerous U.S. and world records and winning gold and bronze medals from the 1924 Summer Olympics in Paris. Ederle broke the existing record when she swam the 35 miles from Cape Gris-Nez in France to Dover, England, in 14 hours and 31 minutes. After that feat, she returned to professional swimming and became an instructor.

George Eliot (Mary Ann Evans), 1819–1880

British Writer

E liot chose to publish using a masculine name so that her work would be taken more seriously. Devoutly religious as a child, she grew up to reject the dogma of traditional Christianity. She moved to London, the English intellectual mecca, and began her unconventional, influential relationship with the writer George Lewes. Best known for her epic novel *Middlemarch*, her contributions to the genre of the novel were enormous, her brilliance lying in her ability to convey the struggles of "good," ordinary people between desire and moral intention and action. Fortified by personal experience and keen observation, she explored the culture of the personal ego versus the traditions of the larger community.

Jessie Redmon Fauset, 1882–1961

American writer

Fauset got her start at the NAACP's magazine *The Crisis*, first as a staff writer, then as a literary editor. There she mentored many young writers; Langston Hughes called her one of the "midwives" of the Harlem Renaissance. Her novels reflected her conviction that it was possible to overcome prejudice, but not self-loathing. Her 1929 novel *Plum Bun* centers around a light-skinned artist seeking acceptance in the white circles of the New York art world by "passing" as white; she finds happiness only when she drops the pose. While Fauset wrote from her own literary and artistic background and experience, many were not ready to believe that African-Americans like Fauset and her characters even existed.

DIANNE FEINSTEIN, 1933–
UNITED STATES SENATOR

F einstein became the first woman mayor of San Francisco in 1978, and enjoyed two highly successful terms. She was among the first women to be considered as a vice-presidential candidate for a major party, and was the first woman nominated for the California governorship by a major party. Undaunted by her loss in both competitions, Feinstein was elected to the U.S. Senate in 1992, becoming California's first woman senator. She has earned a reputation for her ability to guide through difficult legislation, including the preservation of national parklands and a ban on semiautomatic weapons.

GERALDINE ANNE FERRARO, 1935–
AMERICAN POLITICIAN

Ferraro is best known as the Democratic candidate for the vice presidency in 1984—she was the first woman nominated for vice president by a major U.S. political party. Based in her legal practice, Ferraro's political career took her to the House of Representatives in 1978, and she was twice re-elected (in 1980 and 1982). Although she and her running mate, Walter Mondale, were ultimately defeated by the Republican candidates, Ferraro's nomination established her permanently as a political pioneer of the women's movement.

VIGDIS FINNBOGADOTTIR, 1930–
PRESIDENT OF ICELAND

A lthough she is best known as Iceland's president, Finnbogadottir's background is a testament to her cultural commitment to her country. Having served on the Icelandic Tourist Bureau, studied the history of Iceland's cultural relations, directed the Reykjavik Theatre Company, lectured on Icelandic culture, and served on the Advisory Committee on Cultural Affairs of the Nordic Council, she is supremely well-equipped to serve as Iceland's cultural ambassador. Finnbogadottir was elected president in 1980, and was re-elected in 1984 and 1988.

ELLA FITZGERALD, 1918–1996
AMERICAN SINGER

Best known for her incredible voice and her expert "scat singing," Fitzgerald was discovered in Harlem at the age of sixteen. The long list of her contemporaries and bandmates has ranged from the Chick Webb band to the Oscar Peterson Trio. She toured Europe and Asia in the mid-1940s and performed in impresario Norman Granz's "Jazz at the Philharmonic" concerts. In addition to touring in America and overseas, Fitzgerald wrote some of her own material, including "You Showed Me the Way" and "Oh, But I Do." In 1958, Fitzgerald performed in a landmark show at New York City's Carnegie Hall with jazz composer Duke Ellington.

DORIS FLEESON, 1901–1970
AMERICAN POLITICAL COLUMNIST

Known for her clear analysis and biting criticism, Doris Fleeson skewered politicians in her syndicated column. The Kansas native was a feminist and supporter of the underdog at a time when Washington, and journalism, were male- and white-dominated. By the time John F. Kennedy became president, Fleeson was at the top of her profession, along with Walter Lippmann and Arthur Krock. She was probably the most feared political commentator. Kennedy quipped that he "would rather be Krocked than Fleesonized." Fleeson used her influence to espouse causes great and small, including the lack of minority reporters in journalism, and she mentored young women reporters.

ALICE CUNNINGHAM FLETCHER, 1838–1923

AMERICAN ETHNOLOGIST

By 1881, Fletcher had begun her research on the tribes of the Great Plains—the Nez Percé, Omaha, Pawnee, and Sioux. Although criticized for her assimilationist views (she held that Native Americans would survive only through making their way as individuals, rather than keeping with tribal traditions), she was acclaimed for her determination and sharp observations. While deeply committed to observing and recording the details of the tribes' lives, she was also criticized for her support of the 1887 Dawes Act, which allotted land to Native Americans for reservations. She coauthored *The Omaha Tribe* in 1911 with Francis LaFlesche, her adopted son.

CLARA SHORTRIDGE FOLTZ, 1849–1934

AMERICAN ATTORNEY

Foltz and her friend Laura de Force Gordon prevailed on California legislators to change existing state laws prohibiting all but white males from practicing law. When the lawmakers obliged, Foltz in 1878 was able to become the state's first practicing female attorney. She proved to be one of California's most able and celebrated lawyers, winning case after case and earning the nickname "Portia of the Pacific." A male attorney opposing her once suggested that she should be at home raising children, to which Foltz replied, "A woman had better be in almost any business than raising such men as you."

DIAN FOSSEY, 1932–1985
AMERICAN ZOOLOGIST

Fossey is best known for her ground-breaking work in the study of gorilla behavior and ecology. Between 1963 and 1985, she patiently observed mountain gorillas in Africa, where she established the Karisoke Research Center in Rwanda in 1967. She published her observations, dispelling the myth of gorillas as violent, fearsome beasts, in her 1983 book *Gorillas in the Mist*. In 1985, Fossey was murdered at her campsite in Karisoke; the crime is thought to have been in retaliation for her crusade against the poaching of gorillas, among other African animals. The Rwandan government now officially protects mountain gorillas.

ANNE FRANK, 1929–1945
GERMAN DIARIST

Frank and her family fled Nazi Germany to Amsterdam in 1933. In 1942, they hid in secret rooms in an office building. There they lived in silence for two years; Anne chronicled their secret life in her diary. Their apartment was discovered in 1944 during the German occupation and they were put under arrest; Anne died in the Belsen concentration camp less than a year later. Her diary was found after the war and was published by her father in 1947 as *Het Achterhuis* (*The House Behind*), and as *Anne Frank: The Diary of a Young Girl*, in the United States in 1952.

ARETHA FRANKLIN, 1942–
AMERICAN SINGER

Dubbed the Queen of Soul, Franklin is probably most widely known for her hit song "Respect." Her remarkable singing career got its start in her father's choir (he was an evangelist preacher) when she was fourteen. Strongly influenced by visiting gospel singers, Franklin was singing professionally and recording by the time she was eighteen. Her albums include "Young, Gifted and Black" and "Live at the Fillmore West," both in 1971. Among her many awards are two lifetime achievement awards, one from the Kennedy Center Honors (1994), the other a Grammy Lifetime Achievement Award (also 1994).

ROSALIND ELSIE FRANKLIN, 1920–1958

BRITISH BIOPHYSICIST

Franklin is credited with discovering two crucial elements of the structure of the DNA molecule. Using X-ray diffraction, she determined that the phosphate groups lie on the outer part of the molecule, and that the structure of the DNA chain is helical. Unfortunately, her remarkable discovery is best remembered as expediting the research of biochemists James Watson and Francis Crick. After that discovery, Franklin went on to publish her work on X-ray diffraction studies of the structure of carbon.

VIRGINIA KNEELAND FRANTZ,
1896–1967
AMERICAN RESEARCH SCIENTIST

Virginia Kneeland graduated second in her class from medical school at Columbia University. In 1920 she married her classmate Angus Frantz, and she later became the first female doctor ever to serve a surgical internship at Columbia–Presbyterian Hospital in New York. She was appointed to the Columbia faculty in 1924, where her research on cancer gained her national renown. Frantz was one of the first to show that radioactive iodine was effective against thyroid cancer. During World War II Frantz discovered that oxidized cellulose could be used in a wound to control bleeding. In 1948 she received the Army–Navy Certificate of Appreciation for Civilian Service.

ANNA FREUD, 1895–1982
AUSTRIAN–BRITISH PSYCHOANALYST

Particularly concerned with the welfare and development of children, Freud, the daughter of Sigmund Freud, made great strides as a psychoanalyst in her own right. She published a number of works on child psychology, including *Introduction to the Technique of Child Psychoanalysis* (1927), *The Ego and the Mechanisms of Defence* (1936), and *Normality and Pathology in Childhood* (1965). Freud fled the Nazis with her family in 1938 and settled in London. In England, she founded the Hampstead War Nurseries and the Hampstead Child Therapy Course and Clinic (1947), which she oversaw after 1952.

BETTY FRIEDAN, 1921–
WRITER AND WOMEN'S RIGHTS ACTIVIST

Illinois native Friedan revitalized the women's movement in the United States with her book *The Feminine Mystique* (1963). In it, she debunked the myth—which she called "the feminine mystique"—that women find complete fulfillment through marriage and motherhood. In 1966, Friedan helped found the National Organization for Women and served as its first president. As NOW became increasingly radical in the 1970s, Friedan distanced herself from it. In 1970, she was an organizer of the Women's Strike for Equality, the largest women's rights demonstration in the United States in fifty years. Friedan's other books include *The Second Stage* (1981) and *The Fountain of Age* (1993).

META VAUX WARRICK FULLER, 1877–1968

AMERICAN SCULPTOR

Despite the acclaim Fuller's work received abroad, it was not popular in the America of her time; its images were too somber for her contemporaries. Fuller and her husband settled happily in Massachusetts, but a 1910 fire ravaged the Philadelphia warehouse that held most of her early work. Fuller pressed on. One piece, *The Talking Skull*, was particularly haunting. Perhaps it was the way Fuller dealt so explicitly with subjects like death that disturbed her critics. But she never backed off from making a statement with her sculpture, and her works are now seen as prefiguring the Black Renaissance.

(Sarah) Margaret Fuller, 1810–1850

American Writer and Intellectual

Fuller received a top-notch education that allowed her to gain entry to the intellectual circles of Harvard University and surrounding Cambridge, Massachusetts, at a young age. After teaching for a few years, Fuller edited the transcendentalist periodical *The Dial* from 1840 to 1842. While in New York as the literary critic for Horace Greeley's *Tribune*, Fuller wrote her feminist book *Woman in the Nineteenth Century* in 1845. While in Italy as a foreign correspondent, she had a child with Count Ossoli and married him, in that order. In 1850 she and her family fled political turmoil in Italy, but their ship was wrecked off the coast of New York's Fire Island. Their bodies were never recovered.

INDIRA GANDHI, 1917–1984
PRIME MINISTER OF INDIA

The daughter of India's first prime minister, Jawaharlal Nehru, Indira Gandhi played a significant role in Indian politics for nearly three decades. During her rich political career she was president of the National Congress Party (1959) and minister of information and broadcasting (1964). She became India's first female prime minister in 1966. In 1975, faced with domestic unrest and accusations of violating election laws, Gandhi declared a state of national emergency, suspending civil liberties and arresting thousands of political dissidents. She was defeated in the 1977 elections, but made a spectacular comeback three years later, and served as prime minister until her assassination by Sikh conspirators in 1984.

Mildred Gilman, 1896–1994
American Journalist

G ilman bluffed her way into high-profile scandals to write colorful stories for tabloids. While attending the University of Wisconsin, she wrote her first novel, *Fig Leaves*. In 1928, she wrote her second novel, *Headlines*, in New York. That year, armed with a forged letter of recommendation from a recently dead editor, Gilman lied her way into her first newspaper job. When she covered one murder case, Gilman posed as a decoy but was not approached; when the killer sent a note identifying her, she quit her job. Gilman published her third novel, *Sob Sister*, in 1931. During Hitler's rise to power, she interviewed Hermann Göring and wrote articles for several magazines.

Ruth Bader Ginsburg, 1933–
American Supreme Court Justice

In 1993, Ruth Bader Ginsburg became the second woman to serve on the United States Supreme Court (the first was Sandra Day O'Connor). Born in Brooklyn, Ginsburg studied at Cornell University (B.A., 1954), Harvard Law School, and Columbia Law School (J.D., 1959). Despite the obstacles she encountered at a time when the legal profession was male-dominated, she became the first tenured female professor at Columbia Law School, and in 1980 was appointed by President Jimmy Carter to the U.S. Court of Appeals. Well respected for her balanced opinions and moderately liberal philosophies, Ginsburg is perhaps best known for her litigation in favor of women's equality.

Maria Gertrude Goeppert-Mayer, 1906–1972

German-born physicist and Nobel Prize winner

Goeppert excelled at physics at the university at Göttingen, Germany. She married Joseph Edward Mayer, an American chemist, in 1930, and moved to the United States after earning her Ph.D. In the U.S. she worked as an unpaid research scientist for several universities. At the University of Chicago, Goeppert-Mayer became intrigued by patterns in the number of nuclear particles in stable elements. She articulated a "shell theory" of electrons orbiting the nucleus while spinning. Goeppert-Mayer won a Nobel Prize in theoretical physics in 1963. Ten years later, she was offered her first paid full professorship at the University of California.

EMMA GOLDMAN, 1869–1940
RUSSIAN ANARCHIST

A modern-day crusader, Goldman was imprisoned repeatedly. After her immigration to the United States in 1885, she led the anarchist movement in attacking the government and was jailed in 1893 for incitement to riot. Her antiwar efforts proved equally illegal: in 1917, she was imprisoned with fellow anarchist Alexander Berkman for conspiracy to violate U.S. draft laws. After serving her two-year prison sentence and paying a $10,000 fine, she was deported to the Soviet Union. She was deported from that country for her loud complaints about Soviet politics and immigrated to England. Her last defiant act was to help the anarchists during the Spanish Civil War.

141

JANE GOODALL, 1934–

BRITISH PRIMATOLOGIST AND CONSERVATIONIST

An internationally acclaimed animal behaviorist, Goodall is best known for her work with wild chimpanzees in the Gombe Game Reserve in Africa. The Cambridge University Ph.D. dedicated herself to her mission for over thirty years; in 1967 she became scientific director of the Gombe Stream Research Center. Published repeatedly in *National Geographic*, Goodall also wrote *Wild Chimpanzees* (1967) and *In the Shadow of Man* (1971). In 1986, she published the summary of her research, *The Chimpanzees of Gombe: Patterns of Behavior*, hoping to facilitate a better understanding of animal–human and animal–animal relationships.

BETTE NESMITH GRAHAM, 1924–1980
AMERICAN INVENTOR

As a single mother (and an imperfect typist) working as a secretary in the 1950s, Graham kept a little pot of white paint in her desk. She needed it because the carbon film typewriter ribbons in use at the time made it almost impossible to erase an error. The business that developed out of her kitchen in solution to this problem— an invention called "Liquid Paper"—boomed. She taught herself chemistry to improve the formula. When she was satisfied with the results, she applied for a patent. Liquid Paper was a local business for years; by 1979, however, Graham didn't need her secretarial job anymore. She sold Liquid Paper to the Gillette Corporation for $47.5 million, plus royalties.

CATHERINE LITTLEFIELD GREENE, 1755–1814

AMERICAN INVENTOR

Eli Whitney's cotton gin was recognized as the single most important American invention of its time shortly after he acquired a patent for it in 1793. It revolutionized American agriculture. However, the original idea for the gin came from Catherine Greene, mistress of a Georgia plantation. She theorized a machine capable of stripping seeds from balls of cotton. Greene supported Whitney financially during the six-month design period and added final touches to the model he eventually made famous. Nevertheless, the patent for the cotton gin was registered under Whitney's name only, and he enjoyed the fame he gained from it, while Greene's name remained obscure.

GERMAINE GREER, 1939–
AUSTRALIAN-BORN WRITER

Educated at the University of Sydney (M.A., 1961) and Cambridge University in England (Ph.D., 1967), Greer has raised some eyebrows in her career. While lecturing at the University of Warwick, Greer wrote *The Female Eunuch* (1970), which asserted that women have been "castrated" and conditioned to accept the timid, passive characteristics of the eunuch. The book became a bestseller in both Great Britain and the United States, and established Greer's name well beyond feminist circles. Greer's later books did not garner the same level of popularity, and her 1984 work *Sex and Destiny* created a storm of controversy among feminists.

SARAH GRIMKÉ, 1792–1873
AMERICAN ABOLITIONIST

A South Carolina native, Grimké was a crusading pioneer in the antislavery movement of the nineteenth century. Sarah, elder sister to Angelina, broke the law in 1804 when, at the age of twelve, she taught a slave child to read and write. Both Grimké girls were punished. The sisters, both persuasive orators, were also the first Americans to overcome the prevailing edicts against public speaking by women. Even though their audiences were often receptive to their message, the sisters faced boos and catcalls from male audience members who felt women had no place in public debate.

Peggy Guggenheim, 1898–1979
American art collector and patron

Marguerite Guggenheim was born into a family of art collectors; her uncle was Solomon Guggenheim, founder of New York's Guggenheim Museum. Educated in Paris, Peggy was destined for the international artistic elite. When she opened her London gallery, Guggenheim Jeune, in 1938, she filled it with art that suited her tastes, with the help of some advice from French artist Marcel Duchamp. At the gallery she showcased such modern artists as Henry Moore and Wassily Kandinsky. When she moved to New York City in 1941, she opened another gallery, Art of This Century, dedicating it to cubism and geometric abstraction. It was here that abstract impressionists such as Jackson Pollock found their early support.

JANET GUTHRIE, 1938–
AMERICAN RACECAR DRIVER

Before she raced in the Indianapolis 500, Guthrie had been an aerospace engineer, a flight instructor, and a pilot. She'd also had thirteen years of road-racing experience when she was asked to test-drive a car for the 500 in 1976. In 1977, she became the first woman to compete in the Indy 500; although she had car trouble in both 1977 and 1979, she finished ninth in the 1978 race. She was one of the first inductees into the Women's Sports Hall of Fame, and her driver's suit and helmet are on display at the Smithsonian Institute.

CLARA HALE, ?–1993
AMERICAN SOCIAL WORKER

As a resident of New York City's Harlem in the mid-twentieth century, Hale witnessed a marked increase in young women addicted to heroin. She decided to devote her life to caring for these women's children, and founded the first official home for babies born addicted to drugs—Hale House. In 1975, it became the Center for the Promotion of Human Potential, America's first black childcare volunteer agency. Over the course of her life at Hale House, Hale nurtured more than 500 children. The Women's International Center devoted the 1993 Living Legacy Award to this legendary champion of the human spirit.

ALICE HAMILTON, 1869–1970
AMERICAN ACTIVIST FOR INDUSTRIAL SAFETY STANDARDS

Hamilton was a major force in improving industrial safety standards in the early twentieth century. After studying medicine, she took a position in 1897 as professor of pathology at Northwestern University near Chicago. Hamilton moved into Hull House, where she learned about radical politics and poverty, taught, and established a well-baby clinic. Later, she became interested in industrial diseases, and began to document cases of lead poisoning. Hamilton's 1910 study implicated seventy-seven industrial processes in the poisoning of nearly 600 workers. New Illinois regulations regarding testing and safety were a direct result of her work.

LORRAINE HANSBERRY, 1930–1965
AMERICAN WRITER

When Hansberry was eight, her family endured threats, curses, and bricks while living in a wealthy white neighborhood—Lorraine's mother kept vigils with a gun. At twenty, Hansberry moved to New York where she met and married songwriter and music publisher Robert Nemiroff. In 1957, she completed *A Raisin in the Sun*, a powerful play about an African-American family much like her own. It was a hit when it premiered in New York in 1959. Hansberry was the first African-American to win the Drama Critics Circle Award (1959). At age thirty-three, she learned she had cancer. Despite her illness, she continued to write and lecture whenever possible. She died at thirty-four, leaving Nemiroff to publish and promote her work.

PATRICIA ROBERTS HARRIS, 1924–1985

AMERICAN EDUCATOR AND POLITICIAN

Harris brought a long, distinguished background in law and politics to her many impressive posts. A 1960 graduate of George Washington University Law School, she went on to teach law at Howard University from 1961 to 1969. She also concurrently juggled an ambassadorship to Luxembourg (1965–1967) and an alternate delegacy to the United Nations (1966–1967). Harris returned to law with a partnership in a Washington, D.C., law firm (1970–1977), even as President Carter made her secretary of housing and urban development. She was the first black woman to achieve cabinet rank.

HARRIET BOYD HAWES, 1871–1945
AMERICAN ARCHAEOLOGIST

In 1896 Harriet Boyd moved to Greece to study at the American School of Classical Studies. After her graduation in 1900, Boyd went to Crete to do field work. That year, she became the first woman to lead an archaeological dig. Smith College hired Boyd in 1900 as a Greek and archaeology instructor. She took regular trips to Greece, where she led excavations at Gournia; in 1908 she published her findings with the American Exploration Society in a paper still considered a definitive study. She left Smith in 1906, marrying British archaeologist Charles Hawes. In 1919, she began lecturing again. After sixteen years at Wellesley College, in 1936 she retired to Virginia with her husband.

LILLIAN HELLMAN, 1907–1984
AMERICAN WRITER

Hellman's success with *The Children's Hour*, a groundbreaking drama about two small-town teachers accused of a lesbian affair, was a staggering achievement for the 1930s. During the McCarthy years she was blacklisted as a Communist sympathizer. She explained to the House Un-American Activities Committee that she would describe her own activities, but would not provide the names of others. She paid for her convictions—work was scarce under the blacklist—but Hellman never regretted her decision. At Hellman's funeral in 1984, Jules Feiffer recalled her stinging 1952 rebuke to the congressional committee: "I cannot and will not cut my conscience to fit this year's fashions."

AUDREY HEPBURN, 1929–1993

BELGIAN-BORN ACTRESS

Born Edda van Heemstra Hepburn-Ruston to a British banker and a Dutch baroness, Hepburn would become one of Hollywood's biggest movie stars. Hepburn began her career as a model and started acting at age twenty-two. Highlights of Hepburn's career include her starring roles in films like *Sabrina* (1954), *War and Peace* (1956), *Breakfast at Tiffany's* (1961), *My Fair Lady* (1964), and *Wait Until Dark* (1967). In 1953, she won an Academy Award for best actress for her role in *Roman Holiday*. In 1988 Hepburn became a goodwill ambassador for the United Nations Children's Fund, and spent her last years helping children in underdeveloped nations.

CAROLINE HERSCHEL, 1750–1848

GERMAN-BORN ASTRONOMER

Her elder brother William made Herschel his apprentice for his astronomical studies in England in the late 1700s. The two maintained a working relationship that extended over half a century and eventually saw Caroline publish several exhaustive guides under her own name. William discovered the planet Uranus and was appointed Astronomer Royal; for her part, Caroline is credited with discovering eight comets and fourteen nebulae. She received a gold medal from the Royal Astronomical Society in 1828. Caroline maintained her scrupulously organized routine of monitoring the heavens well into old age.

EVA HESSE, 1936–1970

GERMAN-AMERICAN SCULPTOR

Having escaped Nazi Germany as a child, Eva attended Yale University Art School. In 1961 she married another artist, but her work was not taken seriously in its own right. Her anxieties were compounded when her husband won a commission to work in Germany. Hesse had nightmares, but began to develop her own mode of expression. More sure of herself, she returned alone to New York, where she found her niche in expressing extreme emotions through mysterious forms. When in 1969 Hesse was diagnosed with cancer, she directed many of her constructions from her wheelchair. The Guggenheim Museum in New York gave a posthumous exhibition of her work.

LORENA HICKOK, 1893–1968
AMERICAN JOURNALIST

In 1933, Hickok decided that her close friendship with first lady Eleanor Roosevelt compromised her position as an objective reporter. Stepping down from her job with the Associated Press, she investigated Depression-era America, uncovering poverty and disease for the Federal Emergency Relief Administration. In 1940, she began work for the Democratic National Committee. Meanwhile, she lived in the White House with the Roosevelts. In 1945, however, her diabetes, which had long made her work more difficult, forced her to retire from her Washington activities. She turned her talents toward biography, and continued to write until her death.

MARGUERITE HIGGINS, 1920–1966
AMERICAN JOURNALIST

With a master's degree in journalism from Columbia University, California native Marguerite Higgins was a dedicated and fiercely competitive reporter. As the *New York Herald Tribune*'s Far East bureau chief, she won a Pulitzer Prize for her coverage of the Korean war. While raising a family with her second husband, Higgins filed early stories on the Bay of Pigs crisis in 1962 and uncovered emerging problems in Vietnam as early as 1963. Her 1965 book, prophetically titled *Our Vietnam Nightmare*, criticizes the American approach to the conflict. While working abroad, Higgins contracted a deadly tropical infection, which ended her life several months later at the age of forty-five.

Anita Hill, 1956–
American lawyer and lecturer

A nita Hill gained notoriety when she publicly accused
Clarence Thomas, a nominee to the U.S. Supreme
Court, of sexually harassing her. Hill was born in Oklahoma
and graduated from Yale Law School in 1980. She worked at
the Department of Education and at the Equal Employment
Opportunity Commission, reporting to Thomas at both jobs.
She left the second position in 1983 to work as a law professor. In 1991, Hill made her famous accusation. The resulting
hearings polarized the nation and forced the issue of sexual
harassment to the forefront of public debate. Thomas was
confirmed in the Senate by a tiny margin. Hill remains politically active as an author and lecturer.

BILLIE HOLIDAY, 1915–1959
AMERICAN JAZZ SINGER

By the time she was sixteen, Eleanora Fagan was dancing in nightclubs and calling herself "Billie." Her first break came when someone asked her to sing. She went on to record and tour with artists such as Count Basie. However, in 1947 her drug problems went public when she spent nine months in jail for narcotics offenses. Her fans welcomed her back in early 1948, but her personal life continued to plague her. More arrests and several unsuccessful attempts to stop using heroin began to take their toll on her career. She died at New York's Metropolitan Hospital from the ravages of her longtime drug and alcohol abuse at age forty-four.

LETA ANNA STETTER HOLLINGWORTH, 1886–1939

AMERICAN PSYCHOLOGIST

Stetter attended the University of Nebraska, and taught until she married Harry Hollingworth and moved to New York City. She earned an M.A. in education and psychology in 1913 and a Ph.D. in 1916, both from Columbia. Hollingworth challenged the popular notion that women were physically and emotionally impaired by menstruation. She tested women and men at all stages of the month for physical and mental functioning, and reported in her dissertation that she had found no difference between the sexes. Hollingworth focused on child psychology in the 1920s and 1930s. She concentrated on bright children, and in 1936 became the director of the Speyer School for gifted children.

Rear Admiral Grace Hopper, 1906–1992

American mathematician

Known to her colleagues as "the first lady of software," Hopper was one of the inventors of COBOL, a milestone programming language. She was a brilliant mathematician who joined the Naval Reserve in 1943. There she helped to design the first large-scale digital computer, the Mark One, a breakthrough aid to ordnance calculations. She coined the phrase "computer bug" to describe errors in computer software function. When she retired from the Navy in 1986, she was the oldest active-duty military officer in the United States. She died in 1992 at the age of eighty-five.

KAREN DANIELSEN HORNEY, 1885–1952

GERMAN PSYCHIATRIST

Horney was a feminist psychiatrist who challenged Freud's theories, particularly his theory of "penis envy," suggesting instead that women had the more fulfilling role in childbearing, and that, if anything, men suffered from "womb envy." Horney also rejected the idea that female sexual development was inferior to its male counterpart. The mainstream psychoanalytic community considered Horney's differences with Freudian theory radical and threatening, but she established a successful private practice in New York and taught at the New York Psychoanalytic Institute. She published *New Ways in Psychoanalysis* in 1939, and, along with Erich Fromm, helped found the *American Journal of Psychoanalysis*.

VINNIE REAM HOXIE, 1847–1914
AMERICAN SCULPTOR

The teenaged Hoxie, an accomplished sculptor whose work overshadowed that of many of her male competitors, was the first woman awarded an artistic commission by the United States government. By virtue of her work on a statue of Abraham Lincoln in Washington, D.C., near the end of the Civil War, the young artist was one of the last people to see the president alive. The statue was placed in the Capitol rotunda despite a firestorm of criticism surrounding Hoxie's selection as official sculptor.

DORIS HUMPHREY, 1895–1958
AMERICAN DANCER AND CHOREOGRAPHER

After more than a decade with the Denishawn dance company, Humphrey left to pursue her own vision in New York City, where she founded a dance studio in 1928. The lessons she gave there paid for innovative performances of avant-garde choreography. Human emotion and the natural world provided inspiration for her early abstract choreography, which shunned conventions such as costumes, plot, and sound. Pressures and restrictions led to the breakup of Humphrey's company in 1940. Afflicted with arthritis, Humphrey was forced to stop dancing, but in 1951 she was hired by the Juilliard School to choreograph and direct her own performance pieces; in 1955 she founded Juilliard's Dance Theater.

CLEMENTINE HUNTER, 1886–1988
AMERICAN PAINTER

Born in Louisiana, Clementine Reuben married Emanuel Hunter and moved into a plantation house. It was to an artist-in-residence, François Mignon, that Hunter turned in her late fifties when she wanted to paint. He became her biggest promoter, and in the 1950s her work began to attract attention. Hunter painted boldly colored images from plantation life. Her preference for painting from memory is apparent in the flat, representational quality of her work, in which realism is subordinate to meaning. She continued to paint until her death at the age of 101.

ZORA NEALE HURSTON, 1901–1960
AMERICAN WRITER

Zora Neale Hurston is best known as the author of the exuberant novel *Their Eyes Were Watching God*. She was born in Eatonville, Florida, the first all-black town to be incorporated, as well as the first to attempt to organize its own government. Hurston left for New York in early 1925 with $1.50 and "a lot of hope." She became Barnard's first known African-American graduate in 1928, and in 1935, she published *Mules and Men*. Academic posts proved difficult for her to win, and her growing conservatism alienated other African-American intellectuals. However, she left the triumphant work of her prime for rediscovery by a new generation of readers.

ANNE HUTCHINSON, 1591?–1643
AMERICAN ORATOR

Hutchinson mounted an unprecedented challenge against the Puritan hierarchy of the Massachusetts Bay Colony in the 1630s. Her teachings charged Puritan religious leaders with putting too much emphasis on external salvation through "good works" and underemphasizing the importance of an inner relationship with God. This challenge to clerical authority led to legal assaults meant to silence her. Her accusers charged her with acting outside the sphere allowed to women by Puritan society. When Hutchinson claimed to have received a direct revelation from God, she was excommunicated. Hers was the first real challenge to religious intolerance in American history.

QUEEN ISABELLA I, 1451–1504
SPANISH MONARCH

Known also as Queen of Castile and "Isabella the Catholic," she is regarded as one of the creators of a more powerful, unified Spain. She married Ferdinand of Aragon in 1469; the pair took the throne of Castile in 1474. The two greater Spanish kingdoms were united when Ferdinand took the throne of Aragon in 1479. Spain benefited enormously from this union; in 1492 Isabella, with her husband, funded Christopher Columbus's voyage to the New World. The breadth of their power, however, also permitted them to launch the Spanish Inquisition in 1478, leading to the violent expulsion of Spanish Jews in 1492.

MAHALIA JACKSON, 1911–1972
AMERICAN GOSPEL SINGER

Renowned as the greatest gospel singer of all time, Mahalia Jackson had many opportunities in the far more lucrative fields of blues and jazz, which she turned down flat. "I don't work for money," she explained. "I sing because I love to sing." In 1937, Louis Armstrong tried to convince her to sing with his band: "I *know* what you can do with the blues." "I know what I can do with it too, baby," she shot back, "and that's not sing it." Jackson sang for royalty abroad, at President Kennedy's inauguration in 1961, and at the 1963 March on Washington. Jackson was generous with her support of aspiring artists, including Aretha Franklin. She died in Chicago in 1972.

Shirley Hardie Jackson, 1916–1965

American Writer

Born in San Francisco, Jackson met Stanley Hyman, whom she married, at Syracuse University. They moved to New York City to launch their literary careers and a family. In 1948, *The New Yorker* published Jackson's most famous short story, "The Lottery." She also wrote semifictional memoirs of her experiences raising her children, *Life Among the Savages* and *Raising Demons*. She wrote several novels, including *We Have Always Lived in the Castle*. She received the Edgar Allan Poe Award in 1961 but died suddenly of a heart attack at the age of forty-eight.

ADA JAMES, DATES UNKNOWN
AMERICAN SUFFRAGIST

James was Wisconsin's most active suffragist, criss-crossing the state to win adherents to her cause. She was nearly deaf, but this did not deter her from conducting her campaigns on behalf of the extension of voting rights to women. James purchased the most sophisticated hearing aids available, turned them on during her speeches from the platform, and then disconnected them before her opponents had the chance to shout her down. It was an extremely effective rhetorical technique. Due largely to her tireless efforts, Wisconsin became the first state to ratify the Nineteenth Amendment, which in 1920 gave women the right to vote nationwide.

SAINT JOAN OF ARC, 1412?–1431
FRENCH VISIONARY AND MARTYR

Also known as the Maid of Orléans, Joan of Arc played a leading role in French history when she convinced the future king of France, Charles VII, to fight the invading English and seize the throne. Dressed as a man, with cropped hair and a uniform, Saint Joan successfully led French troops to victory at the Battle of Orléans in 1429. After the war, Joan was sentenced as a heretic and was burned at the stake on May 30, 1431. Although a second trial in 1456 posthumously acquitted her of all charges, it wasn't until 1920 that she received her canonization.

Georgia Douglas Camp Johnson, 1877–1966

American playwright and poet

One of the most prominent of all black women writers during the legendary New Negro Renaissance period, Atlanta-born Georgia Douglas Camp Johnson was hailed for her passionate and lyrical work. Her circle of friends included such luminaries as W. E. B. Du Bois, Angelina Weld Grimké, Langston Hughes, and Zora Neale Hurston. Johnson's first book of poems, *The Heart of a Woman*, dealt with love and emotion; later work, including *Bronze,* dealt more explicitly with racial issues. Also an accomplished playwright, she wrote works for the theater, including *Blue Blood* (1928) and *Plumes: Folk Tragedy,* which won *Opportunity* magazine's award for best new play of the year (1927).

Osa Johnson, 1894–1953
American photographer

Johnson, a wildlife photographer, conducted a number of pioneering forays into Africa and Polynesia between 1910 and 1937 that make modern jungle expeditions look tame by comparison. During one harrowing encounter in the South Seas, she and her traveling companion were captured by a group of cannibals. Their captors were eventually won over by Johnson's hastily developed photographs of tribe members.

MOTHER JONES (MARY HARRIS), 1830-1930

IRISH-BORN ACTIVIST

This legendary activist, whose career extended over the better part of a century, was a thorn in the side of the American political establishment for so long that she eventually became a symbol for tireless progressivism. In the early twentieth century, she put a human face on the routinely ignored abuse of child laborers by marching scores of young coal miners from the Pennsylvania mines to the exclusive Oyster Bay residence of Teddy Roosevelt. Such explosive media demonstrations were instrumental in heightening public concern over the issue, and stringent national child labor laws were eventually passed.

BARBARA CHARLINE JORDAN, 1936–1996

AMERICAN POLITICIAN AND EDUCATOR

Best known for her eloquent speech advocating the impeachment of President Nixon during the Watergate scandal, Jordan was the first black student at Boston University Law School and the first black (and first woman) in the Texas Senate. She served on the House Judiciary Committee, where she made her famous speech. In 1978, Jordan left the House of Representatives to teach at the University of Texas/Austin. In 1979, she published her autobiography, *Barbara Jordan: A Self-Portrait*. She is known for her work on civil rights legislation and her commitment to the fight against racism and intolerance.

FLORENCE GRIFFITH JOYNER, 1959–1998

AMERICAN ATHLETE

Florence Griffith was born in Los Angeles and began running track at age seven, winning the Jesse Owens Youth Games at age fourteen. She won a silver medal for the 200-meter dash at the 1984 Olympics. In 1987, she married champion jumper Al Joyner. At the 1988 Olympics, "Flo Jo" won three gold medals: for the 100-meter and 200-meter races, and for the 400-meter relay. She also took a silver in the 1,600-meter relay. Her prowess, along with her flamboyant appearance, made her one of the highest-paid sports figures in the world. In 1989, she announced her retirement from track.

FRIDA KAHLO, 1907–1954
MEXICAN ARTIST

Mexican painter Frida Kahlo led a short, difficult life. A bus accident crushed her spine and pelvis when she was a teenager, leaving her with agonizing pain that thirty-five operations did little to ease. She expressed her pain in her painting, creating fantastic, often disturbing images. Devastated that she could never have children, she often portrayed parts of her body opened up to display pain, sometimes including lifeless fetuses or her cumbersome metal braces. In 1953 Kahlo had her first major exhibit. Despite her debility, she attended the opening on a four-poster bed. After her death, her husband and fellow artist Diego Rivera donated her home to the Mexican government, which turned it into the Frida Kahlo Museum.

NANCY LANDON KASSEBAUM, 1932–

UNITED STATES SENATOR

In 1978, Nancy Landon Kassebaum joined the small, select group of women who have been elected to the United States Senate. Kassebaum served as a member of the Kansas Governmental Ethics Committee and the Kansas Committee on the Humanities. In 1975, she joined the staff of Republican senator James Pearson in Washington, D.C. When Pearson announced his retirement, Kassebaum was elected to take his seat in the Senate. A moderate Republican, Kassebaum was quickly recognized for her political activism and her common-sense approach to policy issues. She was appointed to the Foreign Relations Committee in 1980 and was re-elected to the Senate in 1984 and 1990.

HELEN KELLER, 1880–1968
AMERICAN AUTHOR AND LECTURER

S tricken by a devastating illness as an infant, Helen Keller was left blind and deaf. Through years of special education with her teacher, Anne Mansfield Sullivan, Keller learned to read Braille, use a typewriter, and speak. After graduating from Radcliffe College in 1904, Keller became politically active as a socialist and spoke for many causes. She maintained a strong relationship with the American Foundation for the Blind, and became both symbol and fund-raiser for the organization. She wrote many essays and books on her illness and was the subject of the film *The Unconquered* and of the play and film *The Miracle Worker*.

VALERIA IVANOVNA KHOMYAKOVA, DATES UNKNOWN
RUSSIAN PILOT

A fighter pilot in the Great Patriotic War, as World War II is known in Russia, Khomyakova is recognized as the first female pilot in history to shoot down an enemy bomber. She brought down a German Junkers-88 in late 1942, in a dogfight over Saratov, Russia.

BILLIE JEAN KING, 1943–
AMERICAN TENNIS PLAYER

Tennis champion and feminist spokesperson Billie Jean King rose to the top of her profession in the early and mid-1970s, when she broke all previous professional tennis records for women and became a national heroine. King played a heavily publicized tennis match in 1973 with tennis pro and openly male-chauvinist Bobby Riggs. King first presented Riggs with a live, squirming pig, and then proceeded to win the match. By the time of her retirement in 1979, King had won twenty Wimbledon titles, four U.S. Open titles, and the French Open and Australian Open once each.

Jeanne Jordan Kirkpatrick, 1926–

American political scientist and diplomat

Born in Duncan, Oklahoma, Kirkpatrick graduated from Barnard College in 1948 and received her doctoral degree in political science from Columbia University. Although a Democrat for many years, Kirkpatrick was critical of President Carter's foreign policy and became strongly disillusioned with the Democratic Party. Recruited by Reagan during his first bid for the presidency, Kirkpatrick was the U.S. ambassador to the United Nations from 1980 through 1985, after which she returned to her professorship of political science at Georgetown University. Kirkpatrick has written several books on politics, and has remained a politically active Republican since her return to academia.

SOPHIA JOSEPHINE KLEEGMAN, 1901–1971

UKRAINIAN-BORN PHYSICIAN

Kleegman was one of the first gynecologists to incorporate psychological issues (performance anxiety, repression, and stress) associated with fertility into her medical practice. In 1929, she became NYU's first female faculty member in obstetrics and gynecology at the College of Medicine. In 1932 she married John Sillman and began her studies on fertility and conception. She lectured widely on sex education and was the medical director of the New York State Planned Parenthood Association (1936–1961). Her best-remembered contribution was her work on the "Pap smear," which she developed to yield more diagnostic information. She remained active until her death at age seventy.

Sofia Vasilevna Kovalevskaia, 1850–1891

Russian mathematician

Born in Moscow, Kovalevskaia had to concoct a fictitious marriage at the age of eighteen in order to study mathematics. No Russian university would admit women, and females were prohibited from leaving the country without written permission from a father or husband. In Berlin in 1874, she produced three doctoral dissertations to win her degree; she had to present an airtight case to become the first woman ever granted a doctorate in mathematics. She won the degree—and the prestigious Prix Bordin—fourteen years later. It was only after winning this, the highest honor of the French Academy of Sciences, that she was permitted to hold an academic position in her homeland.

NADEZHDA KRUPSKAYA, 1869–1939

RUSSIAN REVOLUTIONARY

Best known for being married to Bolshevik leader Vladimir I. Lenin, Krupskaya published *The Woman Worker* in the years leading up to the October Revolution of 1917. She successfully lobbied for the observance of International Women's Day, which was first celebrated in Russia. Four years after the holiday's first observance, on International Women's Day, 1917, it was the demonstrations of women textile workers—which grew into bread riots—that sparked the Russian Revolution.

MARGARET KUHN, 1905–1995
AMERICAN SOCIAL ACTIVIST

Founder and head of the Gray Panthers, Margaret Kuhn was one of the leaders in the struggle against ageism in the United States. After graduating from Case–Western Reserve University in 1926, the Buffalo, New York native spent the greater part of her career working first for the YWCA and then for the United Presbyterian Church. Having been forced into mandatory retirement in 1970 at age sixty-five, Kuhn met with other retiring friends who wanted to remain socially active—and founded the Gray Panthers, a group that would become a 40,000-member coalition devoted to fighting age discrimination and other forms of social injustice. Kuhn's autobiography, *No Stone Unturned*, was published in 1991.

LUCY LANEY, 1854–1933
AMERICAN EDUCATOR

In 1886, Laney decided to devote her life to providing black children with a top-notch education. She started in a church basement, but within a few years she was overseeing a private school with more than one thousand young black students. Among them was Mary McLeod Bethune, who would later become the nation's premier black educator. Of Laney, McLeod (who had considered missionary work) wrote, "From her I got a new vision: my life's work lay not in Africa, but in my own country."

DOROTHEA LANGE, 1895–1965
AMERICAN PHOTOGRAPHER

Disabled by polio as a child in New Jersey, Dorothea Lange decided on a career as a photographer before age twenty, although she had never owned a camera. She is best known for documenting the plight of those in distress. Lange was hired during the Depression by the Farm Security Administration to document the housing problems of migrant workers. She was devoted to her subjects, photographing them with sensitivity and passion. The resulting book, coauthored with her second husband, was *American Exodus: A Record of Human Erosion*. Lange's photo "Migrant Mother" is one of the most widely recognized images of the Depression.

Julia Clifford Lathrop, 1858–1932

American social worker

Lathop is best remembered for her landmark contributions to the welfare of the poor. Born in Rockford, Illinois, she attended Vassar College. In 1890 she began working at Chicago's Hull House, the settlement house founded by Jane Addams. Lathrop also worked for the Illinois State Board of Charities, where she sought to improve the standards of institutional care for the handicapped. In 1912, Lathrop was appointed head of the Children's Bureau of the U.S. Department of Labor. She also helped pass the Sheppard-Towner Act of 1921, which funded state programs for family welfare. In 1925, Lathrop became an advisor to the Child Welfare Committee of the League of Nations.

EMMA LAZARUS, 1849–1887
AMERICAN POET

Lazarus was an accomplished poet, dramatist, and translator. Her book *Songs of a Semite* defended ethnic Judaism at a time when there was less sensitivity to cultural diversity than there is today. Her sonnet "The New Colossus," five lines of which are reproduced on the Statue of Liberty, hailed the "huddled masses yearning to breathe free." The lines, if not always their author, have gained a permanent place in American popular mythology.

MARY LEAKEY, 1913–1996
BRITISH-BORN ARCHAEOLOGIST

Louis Leakey was celebrated the world over for discovering the skull of the 1.75-million-year-old "missing link" (*Australopithecus boisei*) in July of 1959 in the Olduvai Gorge of present-day Tanzania. It was not until years later that the world learned that Mary Leakey, not her husband, had actually located the skull. A quiet woman, she was content to let her husband assume the mantle of glory. Widowed in 1972, Mrs. Leakey remained in Tanzania as director of the Olduvai Gorge excavations, and eventually earned her rightful recognition as a leading authority on prehistoric cultures and technology.

MARY LEASE, 1850–1933
AMERICAN ACTIVIST

Lease, a mother of four who was admitted to the Kansas bar in 1886, was one of the most gifted orators of her day. A firsthand witness to the collapsing farm economy, she helped to lead the Populist movement that challenged the two-party system in the prairie states. Her stump speeches attacking both Democrats and Republicans during the elections of 1890 became the stuff of legend. Hers was a remarkably effective appeal that helped the Populists catapult to national prominence. Although she herself did not run for office, Lease was probably the first American woman to sway male voters to her cause in large numbers.

ETHEL (LIGGINS) LEGINSKA, 1886–1970

BRITISH-BORN PIANIST AND COMPOSER

Leginska came to the United States in 1913 for her New York solo debut and was extremely well received. In 1918 she began to study composition, and in 1923 she began preparations to conduct. She made her conducting debut in January of 1925 with the New York Symphony. In 1926 she founded the Boston Philharmonic Orchestra, which she conducted until 1927. She also organized the New York-based National Symphony Orchestra in 1932. She was the first woman to conduct a major U.S. orchestra, and the first woman to write an opera (*The Rose and the Ring,* 1932).

DORIS LESSING, 1919–
BRITISH WRITER

Born in Persia (now Iran) and raised in southern Rhodesia (Zimbabwe), Doris Lessing dropped out of high school at age thirteen. To escape an unhappy childhood, Lessing read voraciously, and became a self-educated intellectual. Twice divorced, Lessing moved to London and published her first novel, *The Grass Is Singing,* in 1949. Sometimes deeply autobiographical, her fiction explores the contemporary female persona and incorporates many political and social issues, including the systematic degradation of black Africans that she witnessed as a child. Lessing's other works include the Children of Violence series, *The Golden Notebook,* and her autobiography, *Under My Skin.*

LENA LEVINE, 1903–1965
AMERICAN PHYSICIAN AND PSYCHIATRIST

Born in Brooklyn, Levine graduated from Hunter College in 1923. She went to medical school at Bellevue Hospital Medical College, and in 1927 she married Louis Ferber. They moved to Brooklyn and when they finished their residencies, they set up a joint practice in their home. Lena practiced gynecology and studied psychiatry. Soon she was splitting her time between her gynecological and psychiatric patients and working for the Birth Control Federation of America (now Planned Parenthood). In Levine's lectures and publications, she addressed female and adolescent sexuality, menopause, virginity, contraception, and marital sex. She lived in New York until her death at age sixty-one.

CANDY LYNN LIGHTNER, 1946–
FOUNDER OF MADD

The idea for Mothers Against Drunk Driving came after a drunk driver killed Lightner's twelve-year-old daughter, Cari. Lightner founded MADD in 1980, and directed it for eight years. Its aim is not only to punish the guilty, but to prevent more drunk-driving injuries and deaths through education and outreaches. MADD not only has chapters in every American state, it also has affiliates abroad. Lightner has appeared on television and before Congress, pushing for more stringent laws and harsher punishment. The difference Lightner and MADD have made, and continue to make, is felt across the country through judicial reforms.

Mary Livermore, 1820–1905
American Volunteer

Hearing of desperate conditions in Union camps during the Civil War, Livermore put her children under the watchful eye of her housekeeper and started to work full-time founding chapters of the United States Sanitary Commission. She initiated over 3,000 local organizations in the Midwest, and is given credit for saving General Ulysses S. Grant's troops at Vicksburg from succumbing to an epidemic of scurvy. Livermore supplied such massive amounts of fresh produce to Union lines that a contemporary observer noted that "a line of vegetables connect(s) Chicago and Vicksburg."

BELVA LOCKWOOD, 1830–1917
AMERICAN ATTORNEY AND ACTIVIST

After earning her law degree from National University Law School, Lockwood was admitted to the bar in Washington, D.C., in 1873. Nominated for president twice on the National Equal Rights ticket, she was the guiding force behind a landmark bill that mandated equal pay for male and female civil servants performing the same work. In 1879 she became the first woman to argue a case before the Supreme Court, and she was the person most responsible for women's suffrage being granted in the states of New Mexico, Oklahoma, and Arizona.

AUDRE LORDE, 1934–1992
AMERICAN WRITER

An outspoken member of the lesbian community, Lorde attacked homophobia and discrimination in her essays, poetry, and autobiographical writings. Born in New York, she was a published writer at fifteen. Her first volume of poems, *The First Cities*, was published in 1968. Lorde's moving fight against her breast cancer was chronicled in *The Cancer Journal* (1980), at a time when public awareness of the disease was not as great as it is today. Her commitment to social issues was extravagantly praised—and doubted—by reviewers. Shortly before she died of liver cancer, Lorde was given a new African name: Gambia Adisa—"Warrior: She Who Makes Her Meaning Clear."

AMY LOWELL, 1874–1925
AMERICAN POET

In 1912 Lowell released her first book of poetry, *A Dome of Many-Coloured Glass*. Influenced by Ezra Pound, Hilda Doolittle, and T. S. Eliot, Lowell composed poetry notable for its evocative, sensuous imagery. Her major books of poetry include *Men, Women, and Ghosts* (1916) and the Pulitzer-Prize–winning *What's O'Clock* (1925). Lowell also wrote criticism and a controversial biography of John Keats. She was eccentric both in her work and in her life—she rarely rose before midafternoon and she covered windows and mirrors in black drapes when traveling. Her most impressive poems are love verses to Ada Russell, her untiring critic and life companion.

CLARE BOOTHE LUCE, 1903–1987
AMERICAN WRITER AND DIPLOMAT

Luce had a diversified writing background. She got her start in magazines, writing for *Vogue* and *Vanity Fair*. After she married Henry Luce, she wrote three Broadway plays: *The Women* (1936), *Kiss the Boys Goodbye* (1938), and *Margin for Error* (1939). During the early part of World War II she served as a war correspondent. From 1943 to 1947, she represented Connecticut in the House of Representatives, and in 1953 she became the American ambassador to Italy. The first American woman to hold a major diplomatic post, she served for four years. She renewed her interest in feminism with her 1970 *Slam the Door Softly*.

SYBIL LUDINGTON, 1761–?

AMERICAN PATRIOT

Most grade-school students are taught about the exploits of Paul Revere, who made his famous ride the night before the Battle of Lexington in 1775 to alert Massachusetts colonists to the approach of the British. Schoolchildren should probably hear about Sybil Ludington as well. On the night of April 26, 1777, the sixteen-year-old rode from town to town to tell New York and Connecticut colonists that the redcoats had begun a raid on Danbury. She produced enough volunteers to help repel the British the next day. Sybil's ride covered twice the distance of Revere's. Her hometown in New York was renamed in her honor by grateful residents.

Rosa Luxemburg, 1871–1919
Polish-born Revolutionary

Fleeing the authorities in 1889 in Poland, where she was wanted for her socialist activities, Luxemburg settled in Switzerland. She immigrated to Germany in 1898, joining a leading international socialist organization. She was imprisoned in Warsaw in 1905 for her part in the Russian Revolution. When World War I broke out, she and Karl Liebnecht formed the revolutionary Spartacists; Luxemburg was again imprisoned for her antiwar activities, and was released in 1918. After the failed Spartacist uprising in January 1919, both Luxemburg and Liebnecht were arrested and murdered by German troops.

MARY LYON, 1797–1849
AMERICAN EDUCATOR

When she enrolled at a boarding school in 1817, Mary Lyon was nearly destitute: she had to weave two blankets and give them to the school in exchange for admission. Twenty years later, Lyon founded Mount Holyoke Female Seminary, which was the first school of higher education for women in the United States. It offered a revolutionary (for women) curriculum that included history, science, and math—subjects thought by many to be not only inappropriate but physically and mentally hazardous for "members of the fairer sex."

Madonna, 1958–
Singer and Actress

At first regarded as retro-feminist fluff by critics, Madonna rose to stardom with her second album, *Like a Virgin* (1984), her music videos, and performance in the film *Desperately Seeking Susan* (1985). Camille Paglia, not one to underestimate the self-styled and outrageous "boy toy," considers her the ultimate feminist, combining "a full female sensuality with a masculine political astuteness." Christened Madonna Louise Veronica Ciccone in Bay City, Michigan, and raised mainly by a hated stepmother, the Material Girl began her career as a dancer and model in New York and gradually moved into music.

Winnie Mandela (Nomzamo), 1936?–

South African political activist and social worker

Winnie Mandela became a strong public figure when her then husband, Nelson Mandela, head of the African National Congress (ANC), was sentenced by the Afrikaner government in 1964 to life imprisonment. For the next twenty-two years, she herself suffered at the hands of the repressive regime, being imprisoned and tortured, restricted in her freedom, and constantly harassed. At the same time, she worked for the poor and sick as well as for the cause of freedom. Finally, in 1986, the government lifted its ban on her and in effect gave up trying to keep her—and the ANC—down. Apartheid was ended in 1994.

WILMA MANKILLER, 1945–
PRINCIPAL CHIEF, CHEROKEE NATION

Forced at age twelve to leave her ancestral home in Oklahoma with her family and move to California as part of a government relocation program, Mankiller returned years later and, after becoming active in community affairs, was elected in 1987 as the first female principal chief of the Cherokees. Presiding over 140,000 tribal members with 1,200 employees and an annual budget of $75 million, her goal was Cherokee revitalization through self-sufficiency and pride. Her surname is an old Cherokee military title given to the person responsible for protecting a village.

LILLIEN JANE MARTIN, 1851–1943
AMERICAN PSYCHOLOGIST

A Vassar graduate, Martin taught physics and chemistry for fourteen years, then decided to become a psychiatrist. Twenty years later, she became the first female head of psychiatry at Stanford University. She had to retire the next year, but in 1920 she established a pioneering program at Mount Zion for preschoolers, and by 1929 she had founded the country's first old-age counseling center—all the while running a successful private practice. She taught herself to drive in her seventies, then drove cross-country—alone. At seventy-eight and eighty-eight respectively she traveled alone to Russia and South America. She died after twenty-five years of postretirement work.

ALICE TRUMBULL MASON, 1904–1971

AMERICAN PAINTER

A lice Trumbull painted the first of her "architectural abstractions" in 1928. That year, she married Warwood Mason and suspended her painting for five years to devote herself to her children. She cofounded American Abstract Artists, and later served as its president, treasurer, and secretary. Her works became starker in the 1950s and 1960s, keeping their harmony no matter which side of the frame points up. When her son drowned in 1958, Mason sank into grief but did not stop painting; *Memorial*, painted for her son, is as tightly composed as any of her paintings. After her death, the Whitney Museum gave a major retrospective of her work.

CHRISTA MCAULIFFE, 1948–1986
AMERICAN ASTRONAUT AND EDUCATOR

Sharon Christa Corrigan McAuliffe was a high school social studies teacher when she was chosen in 1985 to be the first private citizen in space. When the United States space shuttle *Challenger* tragically exploded just seconds after liftoff on January 28, 1986, all of its crew members were killed. While the nation mourned the entire crew, McAuliffe's death was felt particularly keenly. She had been chosen for the flight out of approximately 11,000 teachers; the nation's hopes were pinned on her as the representative of the country's educators and as the future of their profession.

BARBARA MCCLINTOCK, 1902–1992

AMERICAN GENETICIST AND NOBEL PRIZE WINNER

Geneticist Barbara McClintock was the first American woman to win the Nobel Prize in a scientific category by herself. She began her career with a Ph.D. in cytology from Cornell University. In 1931, she coauthored a paper that was later considered a "cornerstone of modern genetics." McClintock presented her Nobel-Prize–winning research in 1951, but her theories were ahead of their time. Although the popular view dictated that genes were stationary, McClintock proposed that some genes "jumped" about, moderating the effects of other genes. The field of genetics later caught up with McClintock when other researchers documented the same phenomenon, and she won the Nobel in 1982.

MARGARET MEAD, 1901–1978
AMERICAN ANTHROPOLOGIST

Mead is most widely known for her field research in the South Pacific, particularly in Bali, New Guinea, and Samoa. Her 1928 dissertation *Coming of Age in Samoa* is her most famous book; others include *Sex and Temperament in Three Primitive Societies* (1935) and her memoirs, *Blackberry Winter* (1972). Much of Mead's focus was on young people, and she studied child-rearing patterns in several cultures. She paid close attention to American social patterns as well, and on how they influenced character, adolescence, and sexuality. The Museum of Natural History in New York hosts the annual Margaret Mead Festival of anthropological films in her memory.

Golda Meir, 1898–1978
Israeli Premier

Born Goldie Mabovich in Kiev (Ukraine), Meir moved to the United States with her family in 1906. In 1921, she immigrated with her husband to Israel. An active Zionist, Meir served as ambassador to the Soviet Union, minister of labor (1949–1956), and minister of foreign affairs (1956–1966). She was prime minister of Israel from 1969 to 1974, following Levi Eshkol. She resigned her post, however, under a wave of criticism for what seemed her lack of preparedness for the 1973 Yom Kippur War, when Egypt and Syria unexpectedly attacked Israel.

LISE MEITNER, 1878–1968
AUSTRIAN-BORN PHYSICIST

Meitner is best remembered for her work on the development of atomic energy. In 1918, she discovered the radioactive element protactinium with Otto Hahn in Berlin. Fleeing Nazi Germany in 1938, Meitner settled in Stockholm, Sweden, where she resumed her atomic research at the Nobel Institute. In 1939, she published the first scientific paper on nuclear fission. In addition, Meitner was the first to predict the existence of the chain reaction. Both of these concepts later proved crucial to the development of the atomic bomb. She taught in the United States twice, as a visiting professor in Washington, D.C., and as a lecturer at Bryn Mawr College.

EDNA ST. VINCENT MILLAY, 1892–1950

AMERICAN WRITER

At twenty, Millay gained an instant reputation when her poem "Renascence" won a contest in the annual literary anthology *The Lyric Year*. On her graduation from Vassar in 1917, she moved to Greenwich Village in New York City. "We all wandered in after Miss Millay," Dorothy Parker later wrote. During the 1920s and early 1930s, Millay was at the height of her popularity and productivity. She became more political over time, and wrote more poems that took up causes like women's rights and antifascism.

KATE MILLETT, 1934–
AMERICAN WRITER AND FEMINIST

Arguing that most traditional relationships are determined by the male need to preserve power over
women, Kate Millett's first book *Sexual Politics* (1970)
made her an instant spokesperson for feminists, and a
celebrity as well. Born in Saint Paul, Minnesota, and educated at Oxford and Columbia, Millet is also a distinguished
sculptor. In her first memoir, *Flying* (1974), she explored
lesbianism and the pitfalls of celebrity, and in another, *The
Loony-Bin Trip* (1990), she gave an account of her experiences with bipolar (manic-depressive) disorder. She has also
explored the elements of torture, most notably in *The
Basement: Meditations on a Human Sacrifice* (1979).

GABRIELA MISTRAL, 1889–1957
CHILEAN POET

Mistral was the first Latin American to win the Nobel Prize in Literature. Although her voice was distinctively Latin American, Mistral's topics were universal, and her lyrical, passionate verses, steeped in idealism, found an enthusiastic international audience. Important collections of her work include *Desolacion* (1922), *Tala* (1938), and *Lagar* (1954). Although Mistral is today remembered primarily as a poet, she also served as Chilean consul in a number of European and Latin American posts, taught literature at some of the best schools in the United States, and served as Chile's representative to the United Nations in the 1950s.

JACKIE MITCHELL, 1914?–1987
AMERICAN PITCHER

Mitchell, the first woman ever to sign a contract with a professional baseball club, pitched for Chattanooga in an April 1931 exhibition game against the New York Yankees. She pitched against both Babe Ruth and Lou Gehrig, back-to-back—and struck them both out.

MARIA MITCHELL, 1818–1889
AMERICAN ASTRONOMER

Born in Nantucket, Massachusetts, Mitchell got her early start in astronomy at her father's small observatory. The first female astronomer in the United States, Mitchell received international attention for herself when she discovered a new comet in 1847. Between 1865 and 1888, she was the first astronomy professor at Vassar Female College, where she remained until her retirement. She was also the first woman inducted into the American Academy of Arts and Sciences (1848). The Nantucket Maria Mitchell Association was founded in her honor; it includes a natural science museum, an observatory, and a science library.

LISETTE MODEL, 1901–1983
AUSTRIAN-BORN PHOTOGRAPHER

Fleeing the threat of World War II, photographer and former musician Model moved to New York with her husband, Evsa Model, in 1938. During her first twelve years in the city, she produced some of her most unforgettable images and began her long-standing relationship with *Harper's Bazaar*. Though her work can rely on the impact of its image alone, Model was also interested in manipulating her photographic images. Often depicting middlebrow entertainments like the circus and Coney Island, Model's work was recognized in several solo exhibits, in the Museum of Modern Art's traveling exhibit *Leading Photographers*, and with a monograph of her work in 1979.

MARIA MONTESSORI, 1870–1952
ITALIAN PHYSICIAN AND EDUCATOR

Montessori was a woman who achieved impressive "firsts." The first woman to attend the University of Rome, she was also, in 1896, the first woman to receive a medical degree in Italy. Her earliest work was with retarded children and adults, most of whom had already been written off as "hopeless" cases. Her incredible results with them guided her in the creation of her unique and effective teaching method, which involved guiding students while allowing them the freedom to set their own pace. After fleeing Fascist Italy in 1934, Montessori went on to teach in Spain and South Asia. The Montessori School system is still popular today.

MARIANNE MOORE, 1887–1972
AMERICAN POET

Moore's talent was apparent at an early age; at nine, she wrote to Santa Claus on behalf of her brother and herself: "Dear Saint Nicklus:/ This Christmas morn/ You do adorn/ Bring Warner a horn/ And me a doll/ That is all." Her first book of poetry, *Poems*, was published in London in 1921. Thrust into the public eye, Moore overcame her innate reticence enough to publish another collection, *Observations*, in 1924, which won that year's *Dial* magazine award. The following year, Moore became *Dial*'s editor. During this period, she worked with such modernist writers as James Joyce and Ezra Pound. She published *Selected Poems* in 1935, and won the Pulitzer Prize in 1951.

JULIA MORGAN, 1872–1957
AMERICAN ARCHITECT

Julia Morgan had designed over a thousand buildings when William Randolph Hearst asked her to be the architect for his massive California castle, San Simeon, in 1919. Hearst requested a home that was both "elegant and comfortable" by his standards; price was not a consideration. The publishing magnate provided Morgan with a list of what the house needed: "100 rooms, an 83-foot assembly hall, 31 bathrooms, two libraries, and a garage for 25 limousines." It was Morgan who turned this laundry list into a technically feasible project and ultimately into one of the most famous design and construction projects of the twentieth century.

Esther Hobart Morris, 1814–1902

American suffragist

Morris, an accomplished nurse and a very tough customer, was the first woman justice of the peace in the United States. Nearly six feet tall and weighing about 200 pounds, she made quite an imposing impression on the residents of South Pass City (then the largest city in Wyoming) who brought their complaints before her. Not one of her decisions was overturned—not even the assault and battery charge and fine she handed out to her husband. It was Morris who first floated the idea of Wyoming women winning the right to vote—at a tea party she gave for legislative candidates in her own home in 1869. No women anywhere in the world had this right at the time.

Toni Morrison, 1931–
American Writer

Morrison is a gripping and prolific writer, among America's most celebrated African-American novelists. The delicate, complicated relationship between blacks and whites, and among blacks themselves, is the backbone of most of her writing. Morrison's vivid, incisive language comes through in her unmistakable style. Her honors and awards include the National Book Critics Circle Award for *Song of Solomon* (1977) and the Pulitzer Prize for *Beloved* (1987). Her other popular novels include her 1973 *Sula*, *Tar Baby* (1981), and *Jazz* (1992). She received the Nobel Prize for Literature in 1993.

GRANDMA MOSES, 1860–1961

AMERICAN PAINTER

Born Anna Mary Robertson, Moses, this most celebrated "primitive painter" did not begin to paint in
earnest until well into her seventies. She taught herself to
paint, working primarily from memory. Otto Kallir, a New
York art dealer, discovered her talent in upstate New York
in 1939. Grandma Moses received numerous awards for
her vivid paintings of rural scenes; these included the 1941
New York State Prize for her *The Old Oaken Bucket* and the
Women's National Press Club Award for her remarkable
achievements—President Harry Truman himself presented
her with the prize.

LUCRETIA COFFIN MOTT, 1793–1880

AMERICAN ABOLITIONIST AND FEMINIST

Although she helped establish the American Antislavery Society in 1833 and cofounded the Antislavery Convention of American Women in 1837, Mott was barred from the international antislavery convention in London in 1840 because of her sex. Not surprisingly, she focused most of her future energy on equal rights for women. In 1848, with Elizabeth Cady Stanton, she organized the Women's Rights Convention at Seneca Falls, New York. Among their many progressive activities, Mott and her husband, both Quakers, made their house a stop on the Underground Railroad after 1850.

MOURNING DOVE, 1888–1936
AMERICAN WRITER

The first Native American woman known to compose and publish a novel was Mourning Dove (the translation of her Okanogan tribal name). Born in rural Idaho, she was encouraged by her grandmother to respect the legends and traditions of her forebears. Mourning Dove interviewed friends and relatives and traveled throughout the Pacific Northwest collecting stories. In 1927, *Cogewea the Half Blood: A Depiction of the Great Montana Cattle Range*, was released. Mourning Dove worked ceaselessly to bring to public notice stories and legends that might otherwise have passed into oblivion. Her autobiography, *Mourning Dove*, was published posthumously in 1990.

ALVA MYRDAL, 1902–1986
SWEDISH SOCIOLOGIST AND PEACE ACTIVIST

Alva Myrdal is remembered for her efforts toward nuclear disarmament. She served as Sweden's disarmament negotiator to the United Nations from 1962 to 1973, and as a cabinet minister during the same period. She also wrote and lectured extensively on disarmament. Her books include *The Game of Disarmament*. In 1974 her husband, economist Karl Gunnar Myrdal, won the Nobel Prize for economics; Alva joined the elite club of winners eight years later, winning the Nobel Peace Prize herself in 1982.

NAMPEYO (THE OLD LADY), 1856–1942

NATIVE AMERICAN ARTIST

Nampeyo was thirty-nine when her husband brought home pieces of pots that had been uncovered at the Sikyatki archaeological excavation. She was so intrigued that she went to the site to sketch the designs, and worked them into her own pottery. Nampeyo painted brick-red and black designs, sometimes abstract, sometimes representational. Her legacy lives on as much in her children as in her works. Three daughters, four granddaughters, and two great-granddaughters all became well-regarded potters in the style Nampeyo originated. In her later years, when she lost her eyesight, she threw pots that her daughter then painted. Nampeyo left an art that continues to thrive in the Southwest.

MARTINA NAVRATILOVA, 1956–
CZECHOSLOVAKIAN-BORN TENNIS PLAYER

To reach the top of the women's tennis world, Martina Navratilova not only had to defect from her native Czechoslovakia in 1975, but also overcome emotional upheavals brought on by her expatriation in America. The hard-serving southpaw won a total of 167 singles matches, including those at Wimbledon in 1978, 1979, and 1981 through 1987, before retiring in 1994. The granddaughter of a tennis champion, Czechoslovakian Agnes Semanska, and the daughter of parents also active in the sport, she was a supreme strategist known for her quickness on the court, her dominant volleying game, and her aggressive shotmaking.

ALICE NEEL, 1900–1984
AMERICAN PAINTER

A fter her graduation from the Philadelphia School of Design for Women in 1925, Neel married a fellow art student and moved with him to Cuba. They returned in 1927 to New York, where their daughter died of diphtheria. Neel's husband then took their second child back to Cuba. Suicidal, Neel was repeatedly hospitalized. By 1932 she began painting forthright portraits. She moved to Spanish Harlem in 1938; *T.B., Harlem* (1940), a martyrlike image of a tuberculosis victim, was inspired by her residence there. Neel also painted portraits of famous artists, including one of Andy Warhol. Before her death, she was elected to the National Institute of Arts and Letters.

FLORENCE NIGHTINGALE, 1820–1910

ITALIAN-BORN NURSE

Nightingale is considered the founder of modern nursing, with her emphasis on strict hygiene and prompt, competent care. During the Crimean War, she supervised a unit of field nurses at British army hospitals. Soon her work both in the Crimea and in Turkey revolutionized field medicine. Nightingale received the British Order of Merit in 1907—a first for women. She founded a training school for nurses in 1860, the model on which future nursing schools were based. Her writing includes her 1858 *Notes on Matters Affecting the Health, Efficiency, and Hospital Administration of the British Army*.

ANAÏS NIN, 1903–1977
FRENCH WRITER

All the details of Nin's life, particularly details of her romantic relationships, were dutifully recorded in her journal. Much of its appeal lies in the accounts of her own "erotic awakening" in an era of reaction to the limited expression available to women. She addressed the problem of establishing one's identity in the face of stereotyping, the nature of female sexuality, and the best response to the limitations of personal relationships. With the first installment of her *Diary*, she tapped a broad and appreciative audience. After *Diary*, interest in Nin's previous work became intense, and reissues and repackagings of unpublished material were quite successful. Two volumes of erotica were particularly popular.

ANNIE OAKLEY, 1860–1926
AMERICAN SHARPSHOOTER

Born Phoebe Anne Oakley Mezee, Oakley got her start with guns early in life. By the time she was sixteen, she had bested the famous marksman Frank Butler, whom she subsequently married. Famous for her incredible speed and accuracy in stunt shooting with rifles and pistols alike, Oakley could shoot a playing card into two pieces and hit a dime in midair from 90 feet away. Not surprisingly, she was the main attraction in Buffalo Bill's Wild West Show from 1885 to 1902, and the inspiration for the musical *Annie Get Your Gun*.

FLANNERY O'CONNOR, 1925–1964

AMERICAN WRITER

Flannery O'Connor is known for writing novels and short stories that present an uncompromising and darkly comic portrait of life in the modern South. O'Connor was born in Savannah, Georgia, and educated in the North. She contracted the debilitating disease lupus in 1951 and was nursed at home by her mother until her death. In Savannah, she wrote her most celebrated works, including the novel *Wise Blood* and the short-story collection *A Good Man Is Hard to Find*. Although her body of work is comparatively small, O'Connor is considered one of the most important writers of fiction of the post–World War II era.

SANDRA DAY O'CONNOR, 1930–
AMERICAN SUPREME COURT JUSTICE

Appointed by President Ronald Reagan to the Supreme Court in 1981, Sandra Day O'Connor became the first woman to achieve that position. An outspoken advocate of judicial restraint, O'Connor leans toward the conservative in her politics, although she has not always agreed with the Court opinions of the more right-of-center justices. She graduated from Stanford University School of Law in 1952 and was the Republican majority leader in the Arizona State Senate from 1972 to 1974.

Georgia O'Keeffe, 1887–1986
American Artist

A modernist painter renowned for her depiction of the American Southwest landscape, her flower paintings, and her still lifes, O'Keeffe has won boundless admiration from both amateurs and art professionals for her striking use of color and form. Her 1917 one-woman show at photographer Alfred Steiglitz's art gallery established her as a member of the New York avant-garde artistic scene and led to the formation of a lasting romantic relationship with Steiglitz, whom she married in 1924. She moved to New Mexico after Steiglitz's death in 1945 and lived there until her own death at the age of 98.

ELIZABETH OLDS, 1896–1991
AMERICAN ARTIST

Minneapolis-born Elizabeth Olds is best known for her powerful, socially conscious lithographs. Lithography, which can produce an almost unlimited number of prints of an image, fit with Olds's vision of art as something for all people to enjoy. After traveling abroad and becoming the first woman to win a Guggenheim Fellowship to study painting in Europe, Olds found her subject matter in Depression-era Omaha, Nebraska. Her lithographs of the grisly everyday realities of Omaha's stockyards earned her critical acclaim and a silver medal from the Kansas City Art Institute.

JACQUELINE BOUVIER KENNEDY ONASSIS, 1929–1994
AMERICAN FIRST LADY AND BOOK EDITOR

No woman has been more famous or fought harder to keep out of the public eye than "Jackie O." When in 1963 her first husband, President John F. Kennedy, was assassinated, her life spiraled into legend. In 1968, she married Greek shipping magnate, Aristotle Onassis. Following his death in 1975, Jacqueline Onassis immersed herself in the field of book publishing, in which she worked as an editor until her own death in 1994. From Andy Warhol's famous silkscreen portrait, to numerous biographies, and a constant barrage of journalists, Jackie O. strove to find a balance between popular iconization and a private personal life.

ELIZABETH PACKARD, 1816–1897
AMERICAN ACTIVIST

A husband grows tired of his wife and decides that, rather than go to the trouble of divorcing her, he'll simply have her declared insane and placed in a mental hospital for a few years. Such situations were common, were accepted by the medical establishment, and were completely legal in parts of the United States until Elizabeth Packard contested her confinement to the Jacksonville (Illinois) State Hospital. In a landmark case, she was declared sane in 1864; her husband was prevented from having her recommitted. Her case drew intense national publicity, helped in the reform of existing laws, and started Packard on a career as an activist.

CAMILLE PAGLIA, 1947–
AMERICAN INTELLECTUAL

This radical and sometimes contradictory thinker came into the spotlight with the publication of *Sexual Personae: Art and Decadence from Nefertiti to Emily Dickinson* (1990), a work of literary criticism that focuses on the pagan element beneath the surface of Judeo-Christianity and argues that nature, not civilization, is the enemy. Paglia grew up in Syracuse, New York, and became an English professor after studying under Harold Bloom at Yale. Since her book's success, she has commented on many issues, including feminism and educational reform.

ALICE ELVIRA FREEMAN PALMER, 1855–1902

AMERICAN EDUCATOR

A professor of history at Wellesley College, Alice Freeman became president of the school in 1882. During her six-year term, she raised enrollment and academic standards and established a more solid financial footing for the institution. Although she resigned in 1888, she joined Wellesley's board of trustees; the same year, she married George Palmer. From 1892 to 1895, she served as the University of Chicago's dean of women. She later held a post on the Massachusetts State Board of Education, campaigning for better teacher pay and improved standards and facilities.

EMMALINE PANKHURST, 1858–1928

BRITISH SUFFRAGIST

Emmaline and her daughters Christabel and Sylvia founded the Women's Social and Political Union (WSPU) in England in 1903. Their focus was on radical action to promote women's suffrage. The group marched on Parliament, chained themselves to railings, and in general looked for ways to get themselves arrested. Emmaline had a huge impact on the dawning suffrage movement in the United States. Her prison hunger strikes and other forms of protest received much media attention and were difficult to ignore. Emmaline died on June 14, 1928, shortly after passage of England's second Representation of the People Act, which granted equal suffrage to men and women.

DOROTHY PARKER, 1893–1967
AMERICAN WRITER

Parker is best known for her acid tongue. Her star rose quickly when she returned to Manhattan after completing her education in New Jersey. By the age of twenty-four, she was *Vanity Fair's* drama critic. The seamless gloss of her magazine pieces, short fiction, and crisp, acerbic poems belies the trouble Parker had in producing them. She became infamous for missing her deadlines. Her longest relationship, to actor/writer Alan Campbell, was mercurial. Parker and Campbell, like many other writers of their time, were blacklisted in the 1940s. The last years of Parker's life were sad, but she left behind her unforgettable poetry, prose, and sharp quotes.

CHARLOTTE "CHARLEY" PARKHURST, DATES UNKNOWN

AMERICAN SUFFRAGIST

In 1868, Parkhurst, who spent her career as a California stagecoach driver masquerading as a man named Charley, became the first woman to cast a ballot in a presidential election. Her vote was illegal, of course, but it was not until her death in 1879 that her gender—and thus her historical voting status—were discovered too late.

ROSA LOUISE PARKS, 1913–
AMERICAN CIVIL RIGHTS ACTIVIST

In 1955, Parks was arrested and fined for refusing to give up her seat to a white passenger on a Montgomery, Alabama, bus. That act inspired the black boycott of the Montgomery bus system, which ended in a federal case that declared segregated seating unconstitutional. A year after Parks's rebellion, the buses were officially desegregated. Although Parks lost her job because of the boycott, she relocated to Detroit in 1957 and resumed her sewing and her longtime work with the NAACP. Her many honors include the Spingarn Medal (NAACP, 1970) and the Martin Luther King, Jr. Award (1980).

ELSIE CLEWS PARSONS, 1875–1941
AMERICAN ANTHROPOLOGIST

B orn in New York City, Elsie Clews studied at Barnard. In 1899 she earned her Ph.D. in sociology at Columbia University, and she married Herbert Parsons in 1900. Meanwhile, she lectured at Barnard and taught at Columbia. Her book *The Family* promoted the idea of trial marriage, a fact that political opponents of Herbert Parsons used against him; the next time Elsie wrote something controversial, she published under the pseudonym John Main. Later, she studied the Zuñi, Taos, Laguna, Hopi, and Tewa people in Arizona and New Mexico. Until her death, she conducted research, published regularly, and served as president of the American Folklore Society and the American Anthropological Association.

LOUELLA PARSONS, 1881–1972
AMERICAN JOURNALIST

Louella Parsons was, during her heyday, the most influential woman in the movie industry. Powerful studio heads regarded her with awe, as her column could boost or sink the popularity—and career—of any star. In the thirties and forties, no star could be expected to survive long without her endorsement. Parsons hosted radio programs and appeared in a movie herself. In the late 1950s, her influence waned as the studio system declined in the face of its first serious competition: television. However, Parsons continued to write columns until 1964. She died of a stroke in California after a long illness.

Alice Paul, 1885–1977
American suffragist

This trailblazing activist brought the techniques of British suffragists back to her native America; she was also the author of the first Equal Rights Amendment submitted to Congress in 1923. The so-called "Lucretia Mott" amendment was never passed by Congress. In the 1970s, Paul—by now an elderly woman—supported the later Equal Rights Amendment just as unhesitatingly. That amendment did make it to the state legislatures, but fell a few states short of adoption. Paul died in 1977 and never saw her ideas incorporated into the United States Constitution. The wait continues.

ANNA PAVLOVA, 1882–1931
RUSSIAN BALLERINA

Pavlova changed from a sickly child into a graceful, glamorous dancer in a true ugly-duckling metamorphosis. She graduated from the Imperial Ballet School (St. Petersburg, Russia) in 1899 and was snapped up immediately by the Imperial Ballet. She ascended to ballerina status in 1906, and in 1907 danced the solo choreographed for her in Fokine's *The Dying Swan*, for which she is best remembered. She soon began to tour abroad, and subsequently moved to London where she opened a dance school named Ivy House in 1912. Touring and dancing around the world with her own company earned her recognition as the greatest dancer of the period.

CECILIA HELENA PAYNE-GAPOSCHKIN, 1900–1979

BRITISH-BORN ASTRONOMER

Becoming the first woman professor at Harvard University was no mean feat, but such was the consequence of the enormous contributions Payne-Gaposchkin made to the field of astronomy. She was the first person to confirm that the chemical composition of the stars and our sun were alike. Her further research on the brightness of stars was of great importance in later research on the evolution of stars and the configuration of the Milky Way galaxy.

ANNIE SMITH PECK, 1850–1935
AMERICAN MOUNTAIN CLIMBER

Peck, the first woman to reach the summit of the Matterhorn and the first mountaineer to reach the top of Mount Huascaran in Peru, received almost as much press for her clothing as for her derring-do. Previous female climbers had always worn floor-length skirts. Peck, who realized the ridiculousness of attempting to scale a mountain while one's clothing restricted the freedom of one's legs, would have none of it (she wore knickerbockers instead). She received waves of derisive press, but her achievements spoke louder than the sexist headlines. Peck made major climbs well into her sixties.

FRANCES PERKINS, 1882–1965
AMERICAN SOCIAL REFORMER

Perkins conducted an influential survey of New York's notorious Hell's Kitchen neighborhood while completing work on her master's degree at Columbia. In 1918, she received an appointment to the New York State Industrial Commission; this marked the beginning of a successful government career. She was named to head the board in 1926 by New York governor Al Smith, and held the post under the state's next governor, Franklin Roosevelt. Perkins was a tireless advocate for the health and safety of American workers, women in particular. Her appointment as U.S. secretary of labor in 1933 made Perkins the first woman named to a cabinet post.

Evita Perón, 1919–1952
Argentinean First Lady

Born Eva Duarte to a poor family in Los Toldos, Argentina, she ran away to Buenos Aires at the age of fourteen, where she became a well-known actress and singer before marrying Juan Perón in 1945. When Perón won the presidency a year later, Evita became his unofficial co-president. She helped achieve suffrage for the women of Argentina, instituted educational reforms, and aided the poor. However, the Peróns' promotion of government employment and unionized labor led to high inflation and economic stagnation in this once-wealthy country. Evita died of cancer in 1952 and was mourned throughout Argentina.

MARY PICKFORD, 1893–1979
CANADIAN-BORN ACTRESS

Born Gladys Mary Smith, Pickford is best remembered for her screen career, especially for *Rebecca of Sunnybrook Farm* (1917) and her Academy Award–winning performance in *Coquette* (1929). While she was one of the first true film stars, her career fizzled early. However, she showed a considerable capacity for business; what most people don't know is that Pickford was one of the original founders of United Artists in 1919, with her husband and Charlie Chaplin.

SYLVIA PLATH, 1932–1963
AMERICAN WRITER

Before she graduated from Smith College, the talented Plath spent a month in New York as one of *Mademoiselle*'s "guest editors." After she returned to college, however, she attempted suicide and spent the rest of the year in a mental hospital, where she was given electroshock treatments. This period is recounted in *The Bell Jar* (1962). In 1956, she met and married British poet Ted Hughes. By the time her two children were born, fissures had developed in her marriage, and the couple separated in 1962. In February of 1963, Plath set mugs of milk near the cribs of her children, blocked off the kitchen, and turned on the oven gas. She was thirty.

POCAHONTAS, 1595?–1617
POWHATAN PRINCESS AND DIPLOMAT

Although the exact details of the legendary incident in which Pocahontas saved John Smith's life near Jamestown, Virginia, are hazy, we do know that she helped establish peaceful relations between Native Americans and the English settlers. She married John Rolfe in 1614, assuming the post of cultural liaison and taking the name Rebecca Rolfe; they had a son, Thomas, the following year. In 1616, the Rolfe family traveled to England, where Pocahontas was graciously received by Londoners, including royalty. She fell ill and died before she was able to return home.

EMILY POST, 1872–1960
AMERICAN WRITER AND COLUMNIST

Born Emily Price, Post is best known for her relentless fight against gaucherie of all kinds. Her writing was tailored to guide people out of the most awkward social situations with aplomb. Having gotten her start in fiction, she became renowned for her 1922 *Etiquette: The Blue Book of Social Usage*, originally published under a different title. The book's runaway success made Post famous; her popularity landed her a nationally syndicated newspaper column and her own radio program. She is fondly remembered as the first pioneer of good manners.

HORTENSE POWDERMAKER, 1896–1970

AMERICAN ANTHROPOLOGIST

Hortense Powdermaker was born in Philadelphia to second-generation German-Jewish parents. She began her career in 1919 as a union leader, but soon became interested in anthropology, earning a Ph.D. from the University of London in 1928. She spent ten months in the Pacific Islands and published *Life in Lesu* in 1933. Another of her projects was a study of Indianola, Mississippi, in which she explored the social structures of the town's white and black communities. Powdermaker was a full professor at Queens College. Her most famous work, *Hollywood; The Dream Factory*, criticized the way in which the values of the Hollywood community shaped its movies.

MA RAINEY (GERTRUDE PRIDGETT), 1886–1939

AMERICAN SINGER

Born Gertrude Pridgett in Columbus, Georgia, Ma Rainey began performing at a young age. She married Will Rainey in 1904, and the two toured together for years. The blues became more and more popular in the late 1910s and early 1920s, as did Rainey's popularity. Between 1912 and 1916, she sang with another blues pioneer, Bessie Smith, on the traveling show circuit—the two artists greatly influenced each other. When the stock market crashed, however, blues music went out of style and Rainey's offers dried up. Her voice, sadly, is remembered but not well represented on the scratchy recordings that were made over six decades ago.

JEANNETTE RANKIN, 1880–1973
AMERICAN POLITICIAN

Rankin, a Montana Democrat, was the first woman elected to the U.S. Congress. Her open opposition to U.S. involvement in World War I, however, led to her defeat in an attempt to win a seat in the Senate in 1918. She later said, "I felt . . . that the first time the first woman had a chance to say no to war, she should say it." Rankin returned to the House in 1940; in 1941, hers was the only dissenting vote in Congress's declaration of war against Japan. Later, in 1968, she led the Jeannette Rankin Brigade in a Washington, D.C., protest march against the Vietnam War.

MARY READ, 1690–1720
BRITISH PIRATE

Read took on the identity of "Mark Read" in the early 1700s to gain a position as a merchant seaman. When her ship was taken by pirates, Read fell in with the notorious woman pirate Anne Bonny and Bonny's male lover, Calico Jack. Bonny probably knew of Read's true identity before they went to sea. A jealous and suspicious Calico Jack believed his rival for Bonny's attentions to be male until he found Read sprawled naked on Bonny's bed. That marked the beginning of an open relationship between the two women that no one in their circle dared challenge, until their capture and conviction in 1720.

Janet Reno, 1938–
United States attorney general

The first woman to hold the post of U.S. attorney general was born and raised in Miami, Florida, and graduated from Harvard Law School. Between 1978 and 1992 she served in Florida as the first female county prosecutor. Regarded as a tough but fair attorney, she is known for her advocacy of children's rights. Reno was in the spotlight in 1993 when she ordered the assault on the Branch Davidian compound in Waco, Texas, and anguished over it. Demonstrating incredible candor and fortitude, Reno accepted her responsibility for the raid's outcome.

SALLY KIRSTEN RIDE, 1951–
AMERICAN ASTRONAUT

Ride was the first American woman astronaut, and the third woman astronaut in the world. In 1978, one year after she received her Ph.D. in physics from Stanford University, Ride was selected to be an astronaut. She flew on two space shuttle missions, in 1983 and 1984. She helped the presidential commission that investigated the space shuttle *Challenger* tragedy in 1986. In 1987, she joined the Stanford University Center for International Security and Arms Control as a physicist. In 1989, Ride was chosen to head the Space Institute of the University of California/San Diego.

MARY ROBERTS RINEHART, 1876–1958

AMERICAN WRITER

Having graduated from nursing school in 1896, Mary Roberts married Stanley Rinehart. She put nursing aside temporarily to raise their three sons. In 1903, however, a dip in the stock market caused her to take up her writing, formerly a hobby, with new determination; she became a main source of the family's income. Her light crime novels proved immensely popular. After a wartime stint as a European correspondent, she used her visibility to back economic equality between the sexes. Undefeated by a struggle with breast cancer, she wrote an article for the *Ladies' Home Journal* about her disease and surgery. She died in her sleep at home in New York at age eighty-two.

Iris Rivera, dates unknown
American activist and feminist

Rivera, a Chicago legal secretary, lost her job in 1977 because she refused to make coffee for her employer. Her rationale: "(1) I don't drink coffee, (2) it's not listed as one of my job duties, and (3) ordering the secretaries to fix the coffee is taking the role of homemaker too far." Although she was not rehired, her case resulted in a large-scale protest by Chicago secretaries and generated considerable network news coverage. The activist group Women Employed presented Rivera's boss with a "coffee demerit badge"—a bag of soggy coffee grounds.

Joanne Robinson, 1912–
American activist

I n 1955, Robinson was head of the Local Women's Political Council in Montgomery, Alabama. She got word of a courageous local woman named Rosa Parks who had refused a conductor's request to move to the rear of a city bus and was now in jail. Robinson saw the opportunity to put into action her group's long-discussed plans for a boycott of the city's bus system. She and two students made a clandestine nighttime trip to Alabama State College, where they used duplicating equipment to print thousands of notices advocating a boycott. The notices showed up everywhere, and the historic boycott was on.

ELEANOR ROOSEVELT, 1884–1962
AMERICAN FIRST LADY AND ACTIVIST

Eleanor Roosevelt was born to a prominent New York City family. She was a social worker before marrying her cousin Franklin, a politician, in 1905. After Franklin was stricken with polio in 1921, Eleanor began to work politically on his behalf. She also became involved in the League of Women Voters. When he was elected to the presidency in 1932, she remained politically active, promoting youth employment and championing racial equality. Eleanor advocated desegregation in the armed forces, and traveled extensively during World War II, supporting the efforts of American soldiers. After her husband's death in 1945, she served as a delegate to the United Nations.

ETHEL ROSENBERG, 1915–1953

ACCUSED AMERICAN SPY

At the height of Senator Joseph McCarthy's "Red Scare," during which no one was safe from his allegations of communism, Ethel and her husband, Julius Rosenberg were caught in his net. Julius, an Army engineer, was accused with his wife of supplying information on the atomic bomb to the Soviets in 1944 and 1945. Ethel's brother testified against the couple; he got a fifteen-year prison sentence for supplying the Rosenbergs with information. Ethel and Julius were convicted under the Espionage Act of 1917, and became the first United States civilians to be executed for espionage, despite international protests questioning their guilt and the fairness of the trial.

Ishbel Ross, 1895–1975
American journalist

During an era when journalism was virtually an all-male field, Ishbel Ross wrote front-page stories for the *New York Herald Tribune* on most major news events between 1919 and 1934, including the kidnapping of the Lindbergh baby, the visit of King Edward VIII of England to the United States, and the inaugurations of three presidents. By all accounts, the reporter was fast, tough, accurate, and nearly impossible to stare down. With virtually no academic credentials to speak of, Ross was also an established historical biographer and wrote more than ten books, including *Ladies of the Press* (1936), an account of early female journalists in the United States.

NELLIE ROSS, 1876–1977
AMERICAN POLITICIAN

R oss, of Wyoming, was the first female governor in United States history. She was married to the state's Democratic governor, William Ross; when he died unexpectedly in 1924, party leaders asked her to head the state ticket. She won handily and served a model first term, reducing state debt by over $1 million and improving performance in public education. She lost her bid for re-election in 1926, but was later named the first female director of the United States Mint by President Franklin D. Roosevelt.

CHRISTINA GEORGINA ROSSETTI, 1830–1894

BRITISH POET

Born into a family of considerable artistic and literary accomplishment, Rossetti made a substantial contribution to the literature of the period. Her deep commitment to religion fueled much of her writing and inspired many of her poems and ballads. Her lyrical style is consistent in her work, from her first book of poetry, *Goblin Market* (1862), through her children's stories, such as *Sing Song* (1872). Rossetti's writing also displays a deep melancholy and a sense of the bizarre or fantastic. Her voice was heard not only within her talented family but in the larger writing community as well, although many still refer to her merely as painter-poet Dante Gabriel Rossetti's sister.

WILMA RUDOLPH, 1940–1994
AMERICAN ATHLETE

Handicapped by a lame leg as a child, Wilma Rudolph overcame her disability to become a world-class athlete. She played basketball as a teen, setting a state record by scoring 803 points in twenty-five games. In 1956, she won a bronze Olympic medal as a member of the U.S. 100-meter relay team. In the 1960 Olympics, Rudolph was the most successful track and field competitor, winning three gold medals: one for the 100-meter sprint, one for the 200-meter dash, and one as a member of the 100-meter relay team. A year later, she set a world record for the 100-meter dash.

MURIEL RUKEYSER, 1913–1980
AMERICAN WRITER

Born in New York, Rukeyser was a brilliant writer very early in life: she published her first book of poems, *Theory of Flight*, at twenty-two. She went on to produce more than two dozen volumes of fiction, biography, criticism, translation, drama, and poetry. The feminist currents in Rukeyser's work were remarkable, given the time in which she wrote. In the preface to one of her works, Rukeyser wrote of a kind of "reaching" in poetry that helps both writer and reader "reach that place where . . . we all recognize the secrets." This sense of personal mystery, wonder, and unremitting action pervades the best of her work.

FLORENCE RENA SABIN, 1871–1953
AMERICAN MEDICAL RESEARCHER

Sabin was a true leader in American science. She earned her degree at Johns Hopkins University School of Medicine, where she was a member of the school's fourth class to include women. Later, as a professor and researcher at Hopkins, she was noted for her pioneering work on the development of the lymphatic system. Sabin was elected to the National Academy of Sciences in 1925. After she was passed over for an important promotion in favor of one of her former students, Sabin left Hopkins for the Rockefeller Institute. There, she spent the remainder of her career conducting valuable research on tuberculosis.

Sacajawea, 1784?–1812
American guide

She was born in what would later become either western Montana or eastern Idaho sometime around 1784. In late 1800, this Shoshone woman was kidnapped by a band of Minnetaree who eventually traded her to a French trapper. She later served as a guide, interpreter, and envoy for Lewis and Clark on their legendary expedition. Her aid in selecting the most direct routes and in securing horses for the explorers to use in crossing the Rocky Mountains was essential to the success of the mission.

NELLY SACHS, 1891–1970

GERMAN-JEWISH POET

The Holocaust was a historic event that altered Sachs's life, and it was her account of it in poetry that earned her, in 1966, the Nobel Prize in Literature. Until the Nazis threatened to put her in a labor camp in 1940 and she fled to Sweden, Sachs wrote formal, neo-Romantic verse about nature. By the end of World War II, she was writing in an entirely different manner, giving a voice to the millions of Jews executed in the camps. Her new work began with bitter laments and grew into poetry of peace and reconciliation.

RUTH ST. DENIS, 1879–1968

AMERICAN DANCER

After building her reputation with a three-year solo tour of Europe, St. Denis met and married Ted Shawn. In 1915 they moved to Los Angeles to found their dance school and company, Denishawn. Denishawn's students included such later choreographers as Martha Graham and Doris Humphrey. Denishawn flourished, its performances becoming more and more popular. However, in the late 1920s the founders' marriage was coming apart. They separated in 1931 but were able to rebuild an enduring friendship. In the later years of her career, St. Denis moved to Hollywood, where she performed until as late as 1964 as a well-loved icon of modern dance.

ADELA ROGERS ST. JOHNS, 1894–1988

AMERICAN JOURNALIST

On more than one occasion, St. Johns took on top-level officials in the Los Angeles city government and exposed widespread corruption among their top ranks. To bring to light LA's neglect of its poor, St. Johns once borrowed a costume from MGM's studios and disguised herself as an impoverished woman in search of employment. St. Johns covered some of the biggest stories of the twentieth century: the Lindbergh kidnapping trial, Edward VIII's abdication and marriage to American-born Wallis Simpson, and even the Patty Hearst ordeal in 1976.

SUSANNA MEDORA SALTER, 1860–1961

AMERICAN POLITICIAN

On April 4, 1887, Susanna Salter went to cast her vote in the local Argonia, Kansas, elections, and was stunned by what she read at the polls. Salter found her own name on the ballot as a candidate for mayor, although she had never expressed any intention to run for the office. Unbeknownst to her, a local women's temperance organization had nominated her and had somehow overlooked telling the candidate of her status. Salter—who had not campaigned—carried the town handily and was thus elected the first woman mayor in the United States. She served for one year.

Deborah Sampson, 1760–1827

American soldier

Sampson was the first woman to enlist in the American armed forces. Under the name Robert Shurtlieff, she disguised herself as a man to serve in the Fourth Massachusetts Regiment in 1782 during the Revolutionary War. She was twice wounded in battle, first by a saber in a skirmish near Tarrytown, New York, and then by a musket shot near East Chester. The second wound was serious, but she attended to it herself rather than risk revealing her true identity. She was awarded a full pension from Congress in September of 1818. Today a monument to her stands in her hometown of Sharon, Massachusetts.

George Sand, 1804–1876
French writer

Sand's writing focuses on the independence and emotional freedom of women. Born Amandine Aurore Lucie Dupin, she left her husband, Baron Dudevant, and moved to Paris to support herself and her two children with her writing. Sand made her mark with her first novel, *Indiana* (1832), in which she set the standard for her infamous iconoclasm by drawing a direct correlation between marriage and slavery. She advocated marriage between equals and championed the working class, openly criticizing the materialism of the bourgeois. Her most popular works include *The Haunted Pool* (1846), *The Country Waif* (1847), and her autobiography, *Story of My Life* (1854–1855).

MARGARET SANGER, 1883–1966
AMERICAN NURSE AND EDUCATOR

Sanger coined the term *birth control* in 1913 in her monthly newsletter *The Woman Rebel*. Her articles on contraception and sexually transmitted diseases led to her indictment for distributing "obscene material"; she fled to Europe, returning when the charges were dismissed. In 1916, she opened a birth control clinic in New York City—and was promptly arrested. She spent a month in prison but emerged as intent as ever on raising women's awareness about contraception. Sanger began publishing the periodical *The Birth Control Review*; birth control centers began to appear in more and more communities. In 1946, with her ideas no longer cause for imprisonment, she founded the International Planned Parenthood Federation.

Sappho, 612 b.c.?–?

Greek poet

Born on the Greek island of Lesbos, Sappho later married and had one daughter. Very little has been recovered of this most famous female poet's work; her nine books of poetry were deemed obscene and burned in the third century b.c. She invented the Sapphic stanza, imitated by Catullus, and the 21-string lyre, which she played to accompany her songs. Famous for her lyrics, Sappho wrote about her passions with a style and sensuality never seen before or since. Most of her love poems are addressed to women, possibly fellow members of a close-knit literary circle.

MAY SARTON, 1912–1995
AMERICAN POET AND WRITER

Sarton finally found critical and popular acceptance when the feminist movement of the 1960s claimed her as one of its own. Writing in both poetry and prose, her main theme was the feminine sensibility. Born in Belgium, she was brought up in Cambridge, Massachusetts, by a mother who was an artist and a father who was a famous historian of science. Some of her numerous works are *Encounter in April* (1937), her first book of poems; *Mrs. Stevens Hears the Mermaids Sing* (1965), a controversial novel now considered a minor classic; and *Plant Dreaming Deep* (1968), the first of her many public journals.

DIANE SAWYER, 1945–

AMERICAN TELEVISION JOURNALIST

Diane Sawyer was born in Glasgow, Kentucky, and graduated from Wellesley College. She began her career as a reporter for a Louisville TV station before serving as a staff assistant to President Nixon. In 1978, she returned to journalism. Highlights of her career include serving as State Department correspondent and serving as co-anchor of *CBS Morning News*. In 1984, Sawyer accepted the position that made her a household name—co-anchor of CBS's *Sixty Minutes*. She left CBS in 1989 for a co-anchor position at ABC's *Prime Time Live*, reportedly for an annual salary of $1.6 million, making her one of the highest-paid women in TV journalism.

Rose Schneiderman, 1882–1972
American activist

At thirteen, she left her job as a clerk in a department store to earn better pay working in a cap factory. Within five years, she and a coworker had founded the first local of the United Cloth Hat and Cap Makers' Union. By 1918, she had become president of the Women's Trade Union League. Schneiderman was a personal participant in every major strike in the textile industry in the first two decades of the century, and was a legendary early organizer of working women.

Patricia Schroeder, 1940–

American congresswoman and women's rights activist

S chroeder received a law degree from Harvard in 1964 and spent several years working in labor relations and as a counsel to Planned Parenthood. She was elected to the U.S. House of Representatives in 1972. Since then, Schroeder has championed liberal causes and women's rights. She strongly opposed the Vietnam War, nuclear testing, and apartheid, and has supported the Equal Rights Amendment, reproductive choice, and the right of women to serve in the armed forces. Schroeder cochaired Gary Hart's presidential campaign in 1984 and considered making a presidential bid of her own in 1988. In 1996, she announced that she would not seek election to a new House term.

SIGRID SCHULTZ, 1893–1980
AMERICAN JOURNALIST

Called the "dragon from Chicago," *Chicago Tribune* foreign correspondent Sigrid Schultz in 1925 became one of the first two women to head a foreign bureau (the other was the charismatic Dorothy Thompson). Schultz is perhaps best remembered for using her considerable diplomatic skills to draw startlingly brutal quotes from top-ranking Nazi officials at dinner parties, including Hitler's right-hand man Herman Göring, and Hitler himself. In Germany she managed to avoid deportation and arrest by pretending to cooperate with German censors while secretly smuggling out stories of Nazi atrocities under a false name. Her book *Germany Will Try It Again* was published in 1944.

Philippa Duke Schuyler, 1931–1967

American Pianist and Composer

Schuyler began writing at two and a half and composing at four. At five she was playing Mozart for audiences, and at ten she joined the National Association of Composers and Conductors. Of mixed parentage, she was celebrated by both the African-American and the white communities, but as she grew up, white America rejected her; Schuyler fled abroad. She changed her name, hoping that a Latin American musician would be better received than an African-American one, but her reviews as a pianist were not good enough to merit much of a career in white America. Her premature death in a helicopter crash was a release from a lifelong search for identity.

FLORIDA SCOTT-MAXWELL, 1883–1979

AMERICAN WRITER

A former actress and psychologist who studied with Carl Jung, Florida Scott-Maxwell set upon the most meaningful work of her life at the age of seventy—when she began writing *The Measure of My Days*. This highly acclaimed journal describing the challenges and triumphs of the aging process debunked negative, stereotypical notions about growing older. "Age puzzles me," she observed. "I thought it was a quiet time. My seventies were interesting and fairly serene, but my eighties are passionate. I grow more intense as I age." She died in 1979, at the age of ninety-six.

ELEANORA SEARS, 1881–1968
AMERICAN ATHLETE

Sears, an accomplished sportswoman who was a four-time National Women's Doubles tennis champion between 1911 and 1917, made headlines when she dared to roll up her sleeves during a match. That was nothing, however, compared with her 1912 jaunt across a field being used for a men's polo team practice. Sears wore jodhpurs and—*scandalous!*—rode astride her horse rather than sidesaddle. A shocked group of local mothers drew up a resolution requesting that she "restrict herself to the normal feminine attire." She ignored it.

HANNAH SENESH, 1921–1944
HUNGARIAN REVOLUTIONARY

The Hungarian government's anti-Semitism in the late 1930s convinced Senesh to become a Zionist at a young age. She moved to Palestine, and when she learned of Hitler's death camps in 1942, she joined a group of British-trained paratroopers. Their mission was to rescue trapped Allied fliers and organize an escape network for those deported to the camps. Senesh parachuted into Yugoslavia in March of 1944 and entered Hungary shortly before German occupation. She was eventually captured, but although she was tortured, she would not divulge any information. Senesh was executed by firing squad in November of the same year. She was twenty-three.

ANNE SEXTON, 1928–1974
AMERICAN POET

Sexton's life is unsettling, perhaps because so much is known about such intimate parts of it. But between drug and alcohol abuse, sexual and physical abuse of her daughters, and physical abuse by her husband, she struggled through seemingly insurmountable odds to become a Pulitzer-Prize–winning poet. The role of a 1950s housewife was an impossible one for Sexton, and she broke down in 1955. She turned to poetry in 1956, and her sharp mind shone through her illnesses and addictions. She was particularly notable as a poet who celebrated female sexuality. But Sexton finally committed suicide in 1974. Like Sylvia Plath, she has since been celebrated as a cult figure.

ANNA HOWARD SHAW, 1847–1919
AMERICAN THEOLOGIAN AND SUFFRAGIST

She entered Boston University's School of Theology in 1876 with one goal: to become a minister. As a woman, she had no access to the financial aid her male classmates enjoyed, but she was able to find preaching assignments outside the school, and was the only member of her class to graduate free from debt. She earned her M.D. at the same institution, and was later ordained. This colleague of Susan B. Anthony was also president of the American Woman Suffrage Association from 1904 to 1915.

MARY WOLLSTONECRAFT SHELLEY, 1797–1851

BRITISH WRITER

Mary Godwin Wollstonecraft was the daughter of writer Mary Wollstonecraft and William Godwin. She married Percy Shelley in 1816; two years later she produced the novel for which she is best known, *Frankenstein, or the Modern Prometheus*. The idea for the book was germinated in an evening's conversation with Byron, one of her literary contemporaries. A deeply philosophical work, *Frankenstein* is unfortunately regarded today as nothing more than a brilliant horror story. Shelley edited her husband's work after his death in 1822, and continued to pursue her own writing, which included *The Last Man* (1826) and *Lodore* (1835).

FRANCES SLOCUM (MACONAQUA), ?–1847

AMERICAN SETTLER

Slocum was abducted during an Indian raid in Wilkes-Barre, Pennsylvania, in 1778. She took the Miami Indian name Maconaqua ("Little Bear"), and was accepted as a member of the community. She married a chief of a prosperous village, raised two sons, and oversaw one hundred head of livestock. Fifty-nine years after her abduction, she was located by joyous family members, who expected her to return to her white origins. Instead, they came face to face with a smiling, gray-haired woman high in the village social order who had forgotten how to speak English and refused to return east with them.

MAUD CAROLINE SLYE, 1869–1954
AMERICAN PATHOLOGIST

Maud Slye was born in Minneapolis, Minnesota, and earned a bachelor's degree from Brown University in 1899. Nine years later, an acquaintance offered her a position at the University of Chicago as a graduate assistant in biology. Slye soon began her life's work on the heredity of cancer with the first of many batches of lab mice. She studied over 150,000 mice over three decades, and found that inheritance did seem to be a factor in determining which mice developed cancer. Slye went on to receive an honorary doctorate from Brown University and a medal from the American Medical Association.

AGNES SMEDLEY, 1892–1950

AMERICAN ACTIVIST

In New York City in 1917, Smedley worked for Margaret Sanger's birth control movement. From 1920 to 1928, she lived in Germany, cofounding the first German birth control clinic. In 1928, she crossed the Soviet–Manchurian border into China, where she taught Mao Tse-Tung to square dance. Smedley also organized medical centers in China and acted as a liaison with the Red Cross. After the war, however, growing anti-Communist sentiment made Smedley a suspect figure in the United States; she was accused of acting as part of a Soviet spy ring. The charges were dropped, but the damage to her reputation was permanent. Her tombstone in Peking reads: "To Agnes Smedley, friend of the Chinese Revolution."

BESSIE SMITH, 1894–1937
AMERICAN BLUES SINGER

Bessie Smith grew up in Chattanooga, Tennessee, where her older sister supported her own child as well as Bessie and her siblings. In her early teens Smith fled Chattanooga for the vaudeville circuit, where she met her mentor, Ma Rainey. By 1920 she was producing her own shows and had enough pull to insist on her own noncommercially plump chorus line—Smith wouldn't perform without them. In 1921 she signed with Columbia Records. In 1937, however, her plans were cut short when her husband, Richard Morgan, crashed the car they were driving. Smith died ten days later in the segregated hospital in Clarksdale, Mississippi.

LILLIAN EUGENIA SMITH, 1897–1966

AMERICAN WRITER

Not many white Southern women of her time were audacious enough to tackle such topics as segregation and prejudice, but Florida-born Lillian Smith was. In 1936 she started the *North Georgia Review,* the first white Southern journal to publish the literary and scholarly efforts of blacks. Smith's first novel, *Strange Fruit* (1944), a daring account of an interracial love relationship, was banned for "obscenity" in Massachusetts. A second book, *Killers of the Dream*, was an unflinching attack on Southern segregation. Though the two popular books established Smith as a writer, many Southerners considered her a traitor to her own people.

Margaret Chase Smith, 1897–1995

American Senator

Margaret Chase was born in Skowhegan, Maine. She married Congressman Clyde Smith and worked as a teacher and a journalist before entering politics herself. She served as a congresswoman for eight years before being elected to the U.S. Senate in 1948—the first woman to be elected to both houses of Congress. Smith served four Senate terms before she lost her bid for a fifth term. She was noted for her intolerance to extremism from both parties, and for her conscientious attendance during Senate debates and votes. In 1964, she became the first woman ever to be nominated for president by a major political party.

CORNELIA SORABJI, 1866–1954
INDIAN ATTORNEY

Sorabji was the first female student at Decca College in Poona, India; when she graduated at the top of her class, she began preparations to attend a British university using the scholarship money reserved for the number-one student. That money was withdrawn solely on the basis of her gender. Shortly thereafter, Sorabji won a fellowship at a prestigious Indian college, and was eventually the beneficiary of a special decree that enabled her to become the first female in India to practice law.

JEAN STAFFORD, 1915–1979
AMERICAN WRITER

After she graduated from the University of Colorado in 1936, Stafford studied at Heidelberg and then settled on the American East Coast. Stafford's intricate short stories were issued in collections as *Children Are Bored on Sunday* and *Bad Characters*. In 1969, *The Collected Stories of Jean Stafford* won the Pulitzer Prize. One of her ongoing themes was illness—sickness or disability represented moral instability; she often portrayed haughty people as neurotic or disingenuous. In addition to novels and short stories, Stafford wrote children's books. She also interviewed Lee Harvey Oswald's mother, and published the results as *Mother in History*.

ELIZABETH CADY STANTON, 1815–1902

AMERICAN ABOLITIONIST AND FEMINIST

The word "obey" was stricken from their vows when Elizabeth Cady married Henry Stanton. Like Lucretia Mott, Stanton was barred from an antislavery convention because of her sex, and responded by throwing herself more energetically into the women's rights movement. She and Mott organized the 1848 Seneca Falls, New York, women's rights convention. Stanton served as president of the National Woman Suffrage Association, which she cofounded with Susan B. Anthony. She also contributed to and edited *The Revolution*, Anthony's feminist weekly paper. Stanton also wrote *The Woman's Bible* (1895) and *Eighty Years and More* (1898), her autobiography.

GERTRUDE STEIN, 1874–1946

AMERICAN WRITER

Gertrude Stein, writer and critic, looms larger than life in stories of the Lost Generation—expatriate artists and writers who populated Paris in the years after World War I. In 1903, Stein settled in Paris. She was a visionary art collector who befriended the artists whose work she bought. Picasso painted Stein's portrait in 1906. Meanwhile, she began to write, developing techniques that sought to intensify experience. Stein's proofreader was Alice B. Toklas, who soon became the primary figure in her life. Stein's writing is notable for its boldly experimental nature, and was not always popular. She never did return to the country of her birth, and died in France in 1946.

GLORIA STEINEM, 1934–
AMERICAN AUTHOR AND FEMINIST ACTIVIST

One of the superstars of the modern feminist movement, Steinem has been an articulate spokesperson for women, both in print and on television, since the late 1960s. Although first regarded as the "pin-up girl of the intelligentsia," Steinem changed her image from frivolous to formidable during the early 1970s and became one of the leading voices for feminist politics and activism. She helped cofound *Ms.* magazine, the influential chronicle of the women's movement, in 1972. Steinem has written a variety of articles and books on the issues that face modern women, and remains an active presence in the feminist community.

Nettie Maria Stevens, 1861–1912

American Biologist

In 1897 Stevens became a thirty-five-year-old freshman at Stanford. She earned a bachelor's degree in 1899 and a master's degree in 1900. Stevens then moved back east to earn her doctorate at Bryn Mawr College. The links between chromosome activity and heredity were first explicitly linked in 1905 when she documented the difference between male and female chromosomes. In 1935 she published the paper that first connected the number of chromosomes with the sex of the organism. Her theory was better accepted when later presented by Edmund Wilson, who arrived at the same conclusions some time after Stevens's untimely death of breast cancer in 1912.

LUCY STONE, 1818–1893

AMERICAN SUFFRAGIST

Stone, pioneering activist and editor of the influential suffragist newspaper the *Woman's Journal*, carried her egalitarian convictions into her personal life. She composed a then-unheard-of document she called a marriage contract with her future husband, Henry Blackwell, in which the pair defined themselves as equals. She then had the audacity to refer to herself as "Mrs. Stone" after marriage. Those women who followed her example were blithely referred to as "Lucy Stoners." A graduate of Oberlin College, Stone cofounded the American Woman Suffrage Association in 1869.

Marie Stopes, 1880–1958
British Social Reformer

The first female member of the science faculty at Manchester University, Stopes earned fame as a campaigner for birth control rights in the 1920s. The medical establishment, the Roman Catholic Church, and even the House of Lords arrayed themselves against her. Stopes's emphasis on birth control as a component of sexual fulfillment was remarkable for that day; few people were willing to publicly advocate that women should be freed from the fear of pregnancy in order to live more complete sexual lives. Her countless legal battles brought massive publicity to her cause, mostly negative. Stopes's books on contraceptive techniques, at first suppressed for being "obscene," eventually sold spectacularly.

HARRIET BEECHER STOWE, 1811–1896

AMERICAN WRITER AND ABOLITIONIST

Living in Cincinnati, Ohio, Stowe was close enough to Kentucky (then a slave state) to observe slavery and the antislavery movement. Drawing on personal experience, Stowe wrote the highly controversial *Uncle Tom's Cabin* in 1852. After the publication of the novel, she remained active in the antislavery movement, lecturing in the United States and abroad. She also published a follow-up account of how *Cabin* was written, and the facts on which she based it, in her 1853 *The Key to Uncle Tom's Cabin*. Stowe was also the author of several other works, including poetry, biographies, and travel logs.

Louisa Ann Swain,
Dates Unknown
American Suffragist

Wyoming's women were the first in any state or territory to gain the legal right to vote; the frontier territory's extension of suffrage to women in 1870 predated the nationwide adoption of the Nineteenth Amendment by fifty years. The first woman to take advantage of the new state of affairs was Louisa Ann Swain of Laramie, who went to the polls early on the morning of September 6, 1870. Swain thus became the first woman to cast a *legal* vote in American history.

MAY SWENSON, 1919–1989
AMERICAN POET

By 1960, Swenson had enough of a reputation as a poet to rely on fellowships to support her writing in New York City. After several volatile relationships, Swenson found her lifetime companion, R. Rozanne Knudson. Evocative poems such as "Year of the Double Spring" won a place in the emerging postwar literary explosion, in which a number of other lesbian writers were being heard. She celebrated physical love and nature as worthy of near-religious intensity and respect. In 1987, near the end of Swenson's life, *The Nation* wrote: "Swenson sees the natural world with startling precision and . . . endows it with a magical radiance . . . . [In] her apprehension of common things . . . she discloses sacred presences."

HENRIETTA SZOLD, 1860–1945
AMERICAN SOCIAL ACTIVIST

Szold is best remembered as cofounder and president of Hadassah, the Women's Zionist Organization of America, in 1912. Hadassah's primary goal was to improve the level of health care in Palestine (now Israel). Szold also became the first female member of the World Zionist executive council. After 1920, she lived in Palestine and worked for peaceful relations between Arabs and Jews. She is also remembered for her commitment to rescuing Jewish children from the Holocaust.

Ida M. Tarbell, 1857–1944
American Writer

Tarbell was one of the original muckrakers. On graduation from Allegheny College in 1880—the only woman in a class of forty—she found little to challenge her, and supported herself by teaching. Tarbell began to research the Standard Oil Company, and uncovered and wrote about a long-standing arrangement between Standard and local railroads that gave Standard breaks on freight prices. Her 1911 book *The Tariff in Our Time* got the attention of President Woodrow Wilson, who in 1916 asked her to serve on the Federal Tariff Commission. She published on many topics into her eighties, including a 1926 interview with Mussolini and an autobiography, *All in the Day's Work*, in 1939.

HELEN BROOKE TAUSSIG,
1898–1986

AMERICAN PHYSICIAN

"**B**lue babies"—babies who come into the world processing oxygen inefficiently due to constriction in a key artery between the heart and lungs—are now much more likely to live since the introduction of the Blalock-Taussig operation in 1945. Dr. Alfred Blalock perfected the technique's execution; the initial idea—which involves creating a new vessel—was Dr. Taussig's. Blalock-Taussig laid the groundwork for most of today's cardiac surgery. Dr. Taussig's operation, which has saved the lives of untold thousands of babies, earned her the Medal of Freedom, the highest civilian honor an American president can bestow.

ANNA EDSON TAYLOR, DATES UNKNOWN
AMERICAN EDUCATOR

The first person to go over Niagara Falls in a barrel and live was a woman. Annie Taylor, a Michigan teacher who couldn't swim, pulled it off in October of 1901. There were many tourists in the area at that time, and Taylor's heavily promoted dive was a hot ticket. The local coroner showed up and tried to persuade Taylor not to go over Horseshoe Falls. Her response: "If the authorities stop my attempt, I will jump to my death over the Falls and you will have work for sure." She suffered bruises and some bleeding, but no broken bones. Six other people have since attempted the feat (all men); only three have lived to tell the tale.

MOTHER TERESA, 1910–1997
ALBANIAN-BORN NUN AND MISSIONARY

Teresa was head of a Roman Catholic high school in Calcutta when the plight of the city's poor and sick moved her to resign her post in the convent to rescue the city's desperate citizens. She created homes for them where they could die with dignity and in peace. In 1950, she and those who joined her were officially recognized as the Missionaries of Charity. Most recently, there were 700 multinational sisters of the order, working on five continents. In 1979, she was awarded the Nobel Peace Prize.

Valentina Tereshkova, 1937–
Russian astronaut

In 1963, Tereshkova became the first female space traveler. She orbited the globe forty-eight times aboard the Soviet craft *Vostok 6*. Her orbit total exceeded that of the six male American astronauts who had accomplished earth orbit to that point. Tereshkova was selected for her history-making flight when Tatyana Tochillova, the country's first choice, failed a preflight physical. Once Tereshkova made her mark on the aerospace world, she served her country primarily as a celebrity. The USSR, having achieved its public relations coup, would not send another woman into space until 1982. The United States would not launch the space shuttle flight carrying American astronaut Sally Ride until 1983.

MARY CHURCH TERRELL, 1863–1954

AMERICAN EDUCATOR AND ACTIVIST

Terrell is credited with the "opening" of Washington, D.C., to people of color. She is best known as the cofounder and president (1896–1901) of the National Association of Colored Women. In 1953, Terrell also led a group demanding the implementation of antidiscrimination laws in D.C. restaurants. The Supreme Court favored Terrell in a landmark case against segregation. In addition to her activism, she also taught and was the first black woman elected to the Board of Education, on which she served for eleven years.

TWYLA THARP, 1941–
AMERICAN DANCER AND CHOREOGRAPHER

Tharp is best known for her ground-breaking dance style, a combination of such forms as jazz, tap, and ballet. She formed her own group, Deuce Coupe, for the Joffrey Ballet in 1973. Tharp choreographed the first American production created for Russian dancer Mikhail Baryshnikov, *Push Comes to Shove*, in 1976, at the American Ballet Theatre; she joined ABT as a resident choreographer in 1988. She has also choreographed several films, including 1984's hit *Amadeus*, and in 1985 she choreographed *and* directed *Singin' in the Rain* on Broadway. Her remarkable and innovative style makes her unique among her contemporaries.

MARGARET THATCHER, 1925–

BRITISH PRIME MINISTER

The first woman to serve as British prime minister (1979–1990) first worked as a research chemist and then as a tax lawyer. Thatcher had always been active in conservative politics, however, and was elected to the House of Commons in 1959. A member of Edward Heath's cabinet, she became leader of the Conservative Party in 1975. Known for her successful stand against the Argentineans in the Falkland Islands conflict in 1982 and for her dislike of welfare-state policies, she promoted a free-enterprise economy and encouraged privatization of nationalized industries. She was the first British prime minister to win three successive elections in more than 150 years.

THEODORA, 497–548
BYZANTINE EMPRESS

Theodora was an accomplished stage performer who developed numerous contacts within the Byzantine elite. After her travels she returned to Constantinople, where she had grown up, and enchanted Justinian, who was heir to the throne. He changed existing law in order to marry a commoner, and she became empress in 527. She was one of the most powerful women in history, centuries ahead of her time—an activist female monarch who liberalized divorce and inheritance laws and tried to stamp out prostitution in the large cities. After she died of cancer, Justinian accomplished little in the way of new laws.

DOROTHY THOMPSON, 1893–1961
AMERICAN POLITICAL COLUMNIST

Thompson was one of the first two American women to head a foreign news bureau (along with Sigrid Schultz), and her fiercely opinionated and widely read syndicated column, "On the Record," made her one of the most important journalists of her day. A passionate and early anti-Nazi, Thompson nevertheless won a rare interview with Hitler in 1931. Her attacks on him in her articles led to her expulsion from Germany in 1934. Five years later, she was declared one of the two most influential women in the world by *Time* magazine (the other was Eleanor Roosevelt).

SUSETTE LA FLÈSCHE TIBBLES (BRIGHT EYES), 1854–1903

AMERICAN ACTIVIST

As translator for Chief Standing Bear of Nebraska's Ponca Tribe, Bright Eyes (whose Western name was Susette La Flèsche Tibbles) traveled all over the United States in an attempt to bring to light the injustice of government policies toward Native American tribes. Later, she came into her own as a lecturer and aided in the passage of the Dawes Severalty Act of 1887, which granted full citizenship rights to Native Americans.

ALICE B. TOKLAS, 1877–1967
AMERICAN WRITER

Gertrude Stein's celebrated literary career would quite possibly have been impossible without Alice B. Toklas—who served as Stein's lifelong companion, advocate, personal secretary, critic, publicist, and business manager. The persona behind Stein's first—and biggest—success, *The Autobiography of Alice B. Toklas* (1933), this San Francisco native penned *The Alice B. Toklas Cookbook* (1954) eight years after Stein's death. A compilation of the various recipes she and Stein had enjoyed with such figures as Ernest Hemingway, Pablo Picasso, and Henri Matisse, the book was also a recollection of the happenings in their legendary Paris salon during the twenties and thirties.

Sojourner Truth, 1797–1883
American Abolitionist and Feminist

Born into slavery, Isabella Baumfree fled to freedom in 1827 after her "master" ignored the New York emancipation act. She changed her name to Sojourner Truth in 1843, when she had a powerful vision of her spiritual mission. For the rest of her life, she fought for black emancipation and women's rights, traveling and lecturing widely. A powerful orator, she became known for silencing her most stalwart opposition with the passion and eloquence of her speeches. Sojourner Truth is best remembered for her 1851 "Ain't I a Woman" speech.

HARRIET TUBMAN, 1821–1913
AMERICAN ABOLITIONIST

Tubman literally followed the north star when she escaped from slavery in 1849, after which she became a leader of the Underground Railroad. It is estimated that she helped 300 fugitive slaves to freedom. She was a brilliant strategist, changing her route every trip and strictly disciplining her charges, even threatening them with a loaded pistol when they came close to panic or surrender. She was such a menace to slaveholders that the accumulated reward for her capture was $40,000. During the Civil War, she was an army nurse and cook, as well as a successful Union spy. Tubman died with full military honors.

ELIZABETH TUDOR
(QUEEN ELIZABETH I), 1533–1603
BRITISH MONARCH

E lizabeth's life could read as a litany of woes, were it not for her triumph in the face of extraordinary adversity. Cursed by her father (Henry VIII) for being female, left motherless when he beheaded Anne Boleyn, imprisoned in the Tower of London by her half-sister Mary, and declared a bastard and excommunicated by the pope himself, Elizabeth nonetheless took the throne in 1558. With her hard-won power and the welfare of Great Britain in mind, she flatly refused to marry, and ruled for forty-five years. Among her other achievements, she instituted fair trials, as well as a public welfare system.

MARIE TUSSAUD, 1761–1850

FRENCH ENTREPRENEUR

Marie Tussaud, accomplished sculptor in wax, was art tutor at Versailles to the French royal family. When the French Revolution began in 1789, she tried to distance herself from the crown, but was nevertheless imprisoned. She was released in short order, however, and upon her release found herself the sole proprietor of her brother's waxworks. This she built into one of the most profitable entertainment concerns in Europe: Madame Tussaud's Waxworks. The prime attractions were death masks she had taken from the severed heads of revolutionary-era figures such as Marie Antoinette, Charlotte Corday, and Robespierre. The waxworks continues to draw visitors to this day.

Tz'u-hsi, 1835–1908
Chinese empress

Originally a concubine to the Emperor Hs'en Feng, she gained immense power in 1856 when she bore his only son. When the emperor died in 1861, she became ruler of China in all but name; no decrees could stand without the Dowager Empress's approval. Tz'u-hsi handed the reins of power to others in 1889, then led a conservative coup following China's devastating defeat by the Japanese in the 1890s. She fled during the Boxer Rebellion of 1900 but returned in 1901 to institute reforms she had once fought against. These included the prohibition of foot-binding, the legitimization of intermarriage between Chinese and Manchu, and the opening to girls of state educational facilities.

Yoshiko Uchida, 1920–1992
American Writer

The vast majority of the twenty-nine books Uchida wrote during her forty-two year literary career were for children—but they did not lack important content or challenging themes. Her writings were strong statements against racism and compelling accounts of the often tragic Japanese-American story. They gave their readers a sense of what is possible in the face of seemingly overwhelming obstacles, and offered a sense of heritage and history to young Japanese Americans. Uchida's books include *The Dancing Kettle and Other Japanese Folk Tales* (1949), *Journey to Topaz* (1971), *Journey Home* (1978), *Desert Exile* (1982), and *Picture Bride* (1987).

BERTHA VAN HOOSEN, 1863–1952
AMERICAN SURGEON

Bertha Van Hoosen was an accomplished surgeon who devoted much of her career to women's health concerns. She attended medical school at the University of Michigan and opened a private practice in Chicago in 1892. In 1902, she was appointed to the staff at the Illinois University Medical School, where she invented the "twilight sleep" anesthetic (scopolamine and morphine) for childbirth, which killed the pain while allowing the patient to remain conscious. Although Van Hoosen delivered over 2,000 healthy children using this method, most of the predominantly male medical establishment refused to try it. In 1915, Van Hoosen founded the American Medical Women's Association.

Charmion von Wiegand, 1899–1993

American Artist

In her late twenties, von Wiegand found herself unhappy with being a society wife. She began to paint in 1926, and soon divorced her husband. Declining financial help, she worked as a journalist and painted in her spare time. In 1932 she married magazine editor Joseph Freman. After much artistic experimentation, she settled on a style involving collages of paper and cloth. Von Wiegand began to paint Chinese characters into her collages. In the late 1940s she began to study Tibetan Buddhist art, finding inspiration for her work in religious symbolism. She continued to study, write, and produce collages into her eighties.

MARY MARVIN HEATON VORSE, 1874–1966
AMERICAN WRITER

Born in New York City, Mary Heaton married Albert Vorse and moved to Provincetown, Massachusetts. Vorse raised two sons and wrote light pieces, and in 1908 published *The Breaking in of a Yachtsman's Wife*. On the same day in 1910, both her husband and her mother died, and Vorse turned to writing in a serious way to support her family. She attended her first strike in 1912 and reported on labor struggles across the country until 1959. She wrote fluff fiction to support the family, as well as more political articles. Even after she retired, she wrote almost until her death at the age of ninety-one.

ALICE WALKER, 1944–
AMERICAN NOVELIST AND POET

The winner of both the Pulitzer Prize and the American Book Award for *The Color Purple* (1982), Walker was born into a Georgia sharecropper's family. At age eight she was accidentally shot in the eye with a BB gun and, because she could not get immediate care, lost sight in the eye. The traumatic injury led her first to introspection and writing, and then, with a disability scholarship, to college, first at Spelman and later at Sarah Lawrence. Another acclaimed novel, *Meridian* (1976), reflects her participation in the civil rights movement. She went on to write *You Can't Keep a Good Woman Down* (1981) and *In Search of Our Mother's Gardens* (1983).

MAGGIE LENA WALKER, 1867–1934
AMERICAN BANKER

A bank president who is black and female—in 1903 Virginia? Maggie Walker's story is truly an inspiring one. She abandoned a teaching position to study business and accounting, and took a position as executive secretary and treasurer of a charitable organization. She was amazingly successful, turning the nearly destitute concern into a multimillion-dollar operation in a few years. In 1903, she took over management of Richmond's Consolidated Bank and Trust Company. The firm's name changed because of mergers over the years, but the hand at the rudder did not; she chaired the board until her death.

MARY EDWARDS WALKER, 1832–1919

AMERICAN PHYSICIAN AND FEMINIST

A Union army nurse during the Civil War, in 1864 Walker became the first woman ever commissioned as an assistant surgeon. The army later decorated her for her field performance. An active suffragist for her entire career, Walker was openly criticized for wearing "men's clothing" in her lifelong efforts to bring about women's dress reform. She is also known for her crusade against capital punishment, her brief postwar journalistic career, and her book of essays, the 1871 *Hit*.

MARGARET FLOY WASHBURN, 1871–1939

AMERICAN PSYCHOLOGIST

In 1894, Washburn became the first woman to receive a Ph.D. in psychology. Her work earned her membership in the American Psychological Association on her graduation. Washburn moved around from 1894 to 1904, taking positions at Wells College, Cornell, and the University of Cincinnati. When Vassar had an opening for her in 1904 as an associate professor in psychology, she gladly took it. There she wrote *The Animal Mind* in 1908 and was promoted the same year to full professor. She served on the APA's influential council from 1912 to 1914, as its president in 1921, and as the coeditor of the *American Journal of Psychology* from 1925 onward.

DINAH WASHINGTON, 1924–1963
AMERICAN SINGER

Washington was born Ruth Lee Jones in Tuscaloosa, Alabama. As a teenager, she was interested in popular music and spent the next few years switching between gospel music and singing in clubs. The manager at the Garrick Stage Lounge is said to be the man who suggested she take a stage name, and in 1943 Jones began touring under the name Dinah Washington—with the tag "Queen of the Blues." She was a mercurial star; by some accounts she was contentious. One story has her smashing a musician's saxophone; in another, she received candy filled with ground glass. Washington died of an accidental overdose of diet pills and prescription drugs.

WENDY WASSERSTEIN, 1950–
PLAYWRIGHT

Regarded as the pre-eminent theatrical chronicler of changes in women's lives during the rise of the women's movement, Wendy Wasserstein has written plays in a satirical vein. In *Uncommon Women and Others* (1977), five women celebrate the choices freedom has brought them and come to terms with the associated fears. This theme is continued in *Isn't It Romantic* (1983) and in *The Heidi Chronicles* (1988), for which she won the Pulitzer Prize in 1989. Wasserstein, a graduate of Mount Holyoke College and Yale University's School of Drama, was raised in Manhattan, where she was exposed to the stage at an early age.

BEATRICE POTTER WEBB, 1858–1943

BRITISH SOCIAL AND ECONOMIC REFORMER

With her husband, Sidney, Webb was a leading economic reformer and theorist. An activist in labor unionism and social reform when she met her husband, she went on to cofound the London School of Economics in 1895. Maintaining their dedication to social justice, the Webbs were the driving force behind the 1902 and 1903 Educational Acts. Among their many publications, the most famous is *The History of Trade Unionism* (1894). When her husband was named Baron Passfield, socialist Webb refused on principle to be called "Lady Passfield."

Simone Weil, 1909–1943
French philosopher and activist

In the midst of her career as a philosophy teacher, Weil took part in the French worker strikes in 1936. She believed deeply in human dignity and in the idea that through suffering, one draws closer to God—this came through in her life and her work. Despite her delicate health, Weil sought out dangerous conditions; for a year, she worked in a factory and studied the physical effects of industry on laborers. When Germany occupied France, Weil would not eat more than her meager rations, although she had tuberculosis. Despite the brevity of her life, her writing (most of it published posthumously) had an enormous impact on the intellectual community.

FAY WELDON, 1933–

BRITISH NOVELIST

Known for her sardonic depiction of modern-day relationships between men and women, Weldon has written numerous stage, radio, and television plays, short stories, and more than seventeen novels. Wary of stylistic labels, Weldon admits that she usually lies about both her personal history and her motivations for her writing and scorns those who take her too seriously. Her novel *Life and Loves of a She-Devil* was made into a Hollywood film and is probably her best-known work to date. She has been published in more than eleven languages, and her novels and writings are bestsellers in England, America, and across the world.

ALICE STEBBINS WELLS,
DATES UNKNOWN

AMERICAN POLICEWOMAN

Wells was the first official policewoman in the United States. She was sworn in as one of Los Angeles's finest on September 2, 1910. Wells faced a unique and frustrating challenge to her authority, however: citizens were constantly accusing her of stealing and misusing "her husband's badge." The police department authorities resolved the problem by issuing her a new model that read "Police Woman's Badge #1" in large, unambiguous letters.

IDA BELL WELLS-BARNETT, 1862–1931

AMERICAN WRITER

Ida Wells-Barnett is best known for exposing the inequalities facing black Americans. Born a slave in Mississippi, Wells-Barnett became the editor of Memphis's *Free Speech and Headlight* in 1891. When she used the newspaper to protest lynchings, a mob destroyed the offices of the *Free Speech,* and Wells-Barnett was warned never to return to Memphis. She took her antilynching work to New York, and in 1895, penned a history of lynching titled *A Red Record.* Wells-Barnett also helped to found the National Association for the Advancement of Colored People (NAACP) in 1910, though she later distanced herself from the organization because she felt that it was not aggressive enough.

MAE WEST, 1892–1980
AMERICAN ACTRESS

Brooklyn-born Mae West began her career in vaudeville, where her quick wit and vampish style earned her rave reviews. Convicted in 1926 in New York on an obscenity charge for a sexy dramatic performance, West went on to write and star in many Broadway productions, including the notable *Diamond Lil*. In 1932 she moved to Hollywood, where she wrote screenplays (*She Done Him Wrong*, *I'm No Angel*, *My Little Chickadee*) and played starring roles. She is remembered for a few famous provocatively growled lines, including "Beulah, peel me a grape," as well as for a film partnership with W. C. Fields.

Ruth Westheimer, 1928–

German-born sex educator and author

She was born Karola Ruth Siegal to a Jewish family in Frankfurt, Germany. Her parents sent her to a Swiss school at age eleven to protect her from the Nazis; they themselves perished in the Holocaust. After the war, Siegal emigrated to Palestine and became a staunch Zionist. In 1956, she moved to New York, where she became a project director at an inner-city Planned Parenthood clinic and earned a doctorate in family counseling. In 1980 "Dr. Ruth" began broadcasting a hugely successful local radio show, "Sexually Speaking," which became nationally syndicated. She is the author of *Dr. Ruth's Guide to Good Sex* and *Dr. Ruth's Guide for Married Lovers*.

EDITH NEWBOLD JONES WHARTON, 1862–1937

AMERICAN WRITER

Born Edith Newbold Jones to an elite New York family, she married Edward Wharton in 1885; unfortunately, Edward suffered from mental illness, and when Edith had settled permanently in France, they were divorced. *The Age of Innocence* (1920) showcased Wharton at her best, writing about upper-class New York society—it won her the 1921 Pulitzer Prize. Progressive movements were not of great interest to her; her flair was the chronicling of social conventions, and the constriction endured by those who deal with difficult moral issues within strict social roles. Wharton continued writing well into her seventies, and died in France after a brief illness.

PHILLIS WHEATLEY, 1753–1784
AFRICAN-AMERICAN POET

When Wheatley was brought to America on a slave ship, her age was guessed at seven, since she was losing her baby teeth. She was bought by John Wheatley in 1761. As her "owners" were kind enough to allow her into their library, she quickly learned English and was writing poetry by the time she was thirteen. Her classically influenced poetry was praised by John Hancock, Thomas Jefferson, and George Washington. Sadly, however, she died in destitution, and only when her 1773 *Poems on Various Subjects, Religious and Moral* was later reissued was she recognized as the first female African-American poet.

MARY JARRETT WHITE,
DATES UNKNOWN

AMERICAN SUFFRAGIST

White voted in Georgia's elections in the spring of 1920, even though the Nineteenth Amendment did not become the law of the land until August of that year. To this day, no one is quite sure how she got away with it. The records show that she was legally registered to vote in late 1919, but they do not indicate what means she used to persuade officials to list her on the rolls of those eligible to cast a ballot.

EMMA HART WILLARD, 1787–1870
AMERICAN EDUCATOR AND REFORMER

Willard was an early champion of the movement for women's higher education. Her approach and her accomplishments were viewed as quite radical; not only did she insist on the study of philosophy and mathematics for women—previously considered actually detrimental to their well-being—she opened her own schools in New York State. These female seminaries trained hundreds of teachers in Willard's innovative vision. In 1895, the Troy, New York seminary Willard founded in 1821 changed its name to the Emma Willard School in honor of her memory.

FRANCES ELIZABETH CAROLINE WILLARD, 1839–1898
AMERICAN EDUCATOR AND REFORMER

Willard left her teaching position in 1874 to assume the post of secretary of the National Woman's Christian Temperance Union, and was elected its president in 1879. An avid prohibitionist, Willard founded the international Woman's Christian Temperance Union in 1883, and became its president in 1891. She was also an active suffragist, and was elected president of the National Council of Women in 1890. Her best-remembered writings are her 1883 *Women and Temperance* and her 1889 *Glimpses of Fifty Years*.

ANNA WESSELS WILLIAMS, 1863–1954

AMERICAN BACTERIOLOGIST

A nna Wessels Williams enrolled in medical school at Women's Medical College of the New York Infirmary, where she was taught by Elizabeth Blackwell. In 1894, Williams became an assistant bacteriologist in the diagnostic laboratory of the New York City Department of Health, where she isolated a strain of the diphtheria bacillus that was particularly useful in the production of an antitoxin for the deadly disease. The discovery was instrumental in New York's pioneering antidiphtheria campaign. Later, Williams became the first scientist to observe evidence of the rabies virus in the brain tissue of infected animals. This discovery led to a vaccine.

Edith Wilson, 1872–1961
American first lady

Between 1919 and 1921, the United States had a female president—or at least came close to it. When Woodrow Wilson suffered a debilitating stroke in 1919, there was no clear rule on who should assume power when the country had an incapacitated—but still living—chief executive. Lacking such formal dictates, first lady Edith Wilson took that authority unto herself for eighteen months. She controlled all access to the president, reviewed his correspondence, and almost certainly forged his signature on documents requiring presidential approval. Although she denied assuming decision-making powers, those petitioning the president began addressing their correspondence "Dear Mrs. Wilson."

Mary Wollstonecraft, 1759–1797

British writer and feminist

After supporting herself as a governess from the age of nineteen, Wollstonecraft wrote, among other works, her revolutionary *A Vindication of the Rights of Woman* in 1792—a book that has caused her to be remembered as the founder of the British suffragist movement. After her marriage to William Godwin, she gave birth to their daughter, Mary Wollstonecraft (later Shelley). Tragically, she died just days after delivery. Her influence lived on, however, inspiring other women writers and feminists, including her own daughter.

VICTORIA CLAFLIN WOODHULL, 1838–1927

AMERICAN FEMINIST

The first woman to run for the U.S. presidency, Woodhull spent a most unusual childhood traveling with her parents' medicine show before marrying Canning Woodhull at age fifteen. Woodhull and her sister Tennessee collaborated to start a Wall Street brokerage firm, as well as a newspaper, in which they promoted free love and equal rights for women. In 1872 Woodhull was nominated for the U.S. presidency by the Equal Rights Party. In the same year, a sensational scandal erupted when Woodhull claimed in her newspaper that Reverend Henry Ward Beecher had committed adultery. She fled to England, where she remarried and withdrew from public life.

VIRGINIA WOOLF, 1882–1941

BRITISH WRITER AND FEMINIST

Adeline Virginia Stephen was a precocious writer, producing experimental novels using a stream-of-consciousness perspective and publishing incisive essays. Her best-known novels are *Mrs. Dalloway* (1925) and *To the Lighthouse* (1927), and her most famous essay is the feminist treatise *A Room of One's Own* (1929). Unfortunately, her literary success did nothing to bolster her fragile physical and emotional health. Her husband, Leonard Woolf, cared for her tirelessly, but with the onset of another nervous breakdown in 1941, Woolf drowned herself rather than face the madness she so feared. Volumes of her correspondence, journals, criticism, and essays were published posthumously.

FANNY WRIGHT, 1795–1852
BRITISH-BORN ACTIVIST

How radical is radical? In the United States, in 1828, Fanny Wright was about as far on the fringe as you could get. She spoke out against slavery, advocated the right of individuals of both sexes to choose their sexual partners outside of the legal bounds of marriage, and suggested that intermarriage could eventually solve the country's race problem. This was more than the newspaper writers of the day could stand: Wright was branded by apoplectic male observers as a "blasphemer," a "preacher of licentiousness," and a promoter of "vice and sensuality in its most loathsome form."

ELINOR HOYT WYLIE, 1885–1928
AMERICAN WRITER

Wylie released *Trivial Breath* in 1928, showcasing the verses of a disciplined, clear-thinking writer whose life had touched both despair and resolve. Wylie's acceptance of mortality and her pleasure in the world of physical things contain a strange happiness that underlies the collection. Her final collection, *Angels and Earthly Creatures* (1929), features a series of sonnets that constitute meditations on a new, all-consuming love—she was apparently embarking on a new affair when she completed the manuscript. Sadly, complications arising from a serious fall combined with hypertension, and she suffered a stroke in October of 1928, dying later that year.

MILDRED "BABE" DIDRIKSON
ZAHARIAS, 1914–1956
AMERICAN ATHLETE

One of the most outstanding women athletes in history, Mildred "Babe" Didrikson began her career playing basketball, then moved on to track and field events. At the 1932 Olympics, she set two world records and won two gold medals for javelin and hurdles, as well as a silver for the high jump. By 1935 she had moved on to golf. In 1947, she won seventeen amateur tournaments in a row before turning professional. As a professional, Zaharias won three Women's Open titles. Over the years Zaharias tried her hand at baseball, swimming, and figure skating, excelling at each.

BIBLIOGRAPHY

Brooke Bailey. *The Remarkable Lives of 100 Women Artists*. Holbrook, Mass.: Adams Media Corporation, 1994.

Brooke Bailey. *The Remarkable Lives of 100 Women Healers and Scientists*. Holbrook, Mass.: Adams Media Corporation, 1994.

Brooke Bailey. *The Remarkable Lives of 100 Women Writers and Journalists*. Holbrook, Mass.: Adams Media Corporation, 1994.

Lynne Griffin and Kelly McCann. *The Book of Women: 300 Notable Women History Passed By*. Holbrook, Mass.: Adams Media Corporation, 1995.

David L. Porter. *Biographical Dictionary of American Sports: Outdoor Sports*. New York: Greenwood, 1988.

Phyllis J. Read and Bernard L. Witlieb, eds. *The Book of Women's Firsts*. New York: Random House, 1992.

Barbara Sicherman and Carol Hurd Green, eds. *Notable American Women: The Modern Period*. Cambridge, Mass.: Belknap Press of Harvard University Press, 1980.

Edward T. James, ed. *Notable American Women: 1607–1950*. Vols. 1–3. Cambridge, Mass.: Belknap Press of Harvard University Press, 1971.

Current Biography Yearbook. New York: H.W. Wilson, 1945, 1961, 1964, 1967–68, 1977–78, 1984, 1986–90, 1992–95.

Microsoft® Encarta® 95 Encyclopedia.

The New Grolier Multimedia Encyclopedia™. Danbury, Conn.: Grolier Inc., 1993.

Who's Who. New York: St. Martin's, 1996.

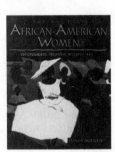